Hopkinsville-Christian County Public Library
1101 BETHEL STREET
HOPKINSVILLE, KENTUCKY 42240

GAYLORD RG

CHARLIE TROTTER'S

MEAT & GAME

Recipes by
Charlie Trotter

Wine Notes by
Belinda Chang

Food Photography by
Tim Turner

Location Photography by
Michael Voltattorni

Ten Speed Press, Berkeley, California

animals

Contents

Light Poultry &
Other Fowl

Robust Poultry & Other Fowl

Light Meat & Game

Robust Meat & Game

Varietal Meat

Traditions and celebrations bring together family and friends to partake in spectacular feasts, the centerpiece often a triumphant dish of meat or game. I have fond memories of tender springtime lamb on Easter Sunday, a magnificent roast on Christmas, and a splendid, juicy turkey on Thanksgiving. These were the festivities of my family and times that I cherish. Meat and game continue to hold a special place at our table. My wife, Lynn, cooks marinated meats on the grill—wonderful meals to come home to and make toasts over—and my son, Dylan, is a chicken fanatic. We enjoy incredible dinners wherever we travel, savoring the meat and game of the region.

Roasting, braising, grilling, poaching, and sautéing are the basics in the myriad of methods to prepare various cuts of meat. Each transforms the flavor and texture of the meat in its own way. A roasted bird, most of the fat rendered, leaving a crispy skin to contrast with the juicy flesh; a lamb shank braised overnight in the oven until the meat falls from the

Introduction

bone; silky chicken poached lightly in buttermilk; and fragrant sautéed foie gras with the outside just caramelized are but a few wondrous ways meat and game make the transition from foodstuff to feast. The smells and flavors of meat have no rival, but their power should harmonize and play off of the other elements on the plate, not overshadow them. At the restaurant, we have always given an essential role to vegetables and grains. Meat is the solid bass line to their melody of textures and flavors.

Similar to our previous explorations of foodstuffs, the recipes found in these pages reflect what is being served at the restaurant. This book is a record of our kitchen's culinary evolution and a testament to what has been created within it. Although the recipes have been meticulously written and tested to create succulent dishes, they should not stifle or limit the creative culinary process. Think of the recipes as interpretations found to be particularly pleasing. Look at these pages for inspiration and fresh ideas, then make

the dishes your own, either by the substitutions we have offered or through the endless possibilities evoked by the foodstuffs themselves.

All of the preparations and techniques used at the restaurant and in this book are grounded in Western European tradition. Long ago, the master cooks of France and Italy perfected the various cooking methods for meat and game. The massive kitchens of kings produced sumptuous feasts centered around the glory of the hunt. The expertise of the cook was demonstrated through the numerous methods of preparing various cuts of meat. While preserving this grand tradition, our recipes have been lightened by an Asian-minimalist influence. Gone are the heavy, cloying sauces, the excessive richness of accompaniments, and the sometimes destructive overcooking.

At the restaurant, we stress the synergy of food and wine as an important aspect of the dining experience. Wine tasting and pairing was a critical component in the creation of every recipe

in this book. The wine selections bring out the flavors of each dish and heighten the sensory experience that is the pinnacle of dining. However, these pairings should in no way hinder exploration of the breadth of wine varietals, regions, and vineyards. Conduct samplings to discover why these wines were suggested and whether any alterations and spontaneous riffs on the recipe change the suitability of a given pairing. Through such trials it becomes evident that the interplay between food and wine heightens the enjoyment of both.

The ritual of slicing a piece of perfectly cooked meat or game, smelling the heady aroma, watching the luscious juice seep onto and flavor the accompaniments, and finally, savoring the robust flavor is one of life's ultimate sensual experiences. As any passionate cook will tell you, creating this experience for others is the true pleasure of the table.

Charlie Trotter

...our ancestors have turned a savage wilderness into a glorious empire—EDMUND BURKE

Light Poultry
& Other Fowl

Sweet-and-Sour Braised Lettuce Soup
with Foie Gras and Radishes

The sweet-and-sour lettuce soup is an ideal medium, both texturally and flavorwise,
for the rich and extravagant flavor of the foie gras. Radish and pearl onion pieces provide another
layer of complexity, as well as additional sweetness and sharpness and some sultry textural notes.
Wisps of chive and droplets of Herb Oil add a playful bite and a necessary herby richness,
respectively. Overall, this dish provides surprise and delight at the same time.

Serves 4

8 red pearl onions

4 red radishes

8 shallots, sliced into thin rings

5 1/2 tablespoons butter

3 tablespoons sugar

1/2 cup rice vinegar

*1 medium head Boston lettuce, cored
and chopped*

4 cups Chicken Stock (see Appendices)

Salt and pepper

*12 ounces foie gras, cleaned and cut into
1/2 inch cubes*

8 teaspoons Herb Oil (see Appendices)

8 fresh chives, finely cut on the diagonal

METHOD To prepare the soup: Cook the pearl onions in boiling salted water for 10 minutes. Drain, remove the skins from the onions, and cut in half. Cook the rad- ishes in boiling salted water for 5 to 7 minutes, or until tender. Drain and thinly slice.

Place the shallots in a large saucepan with 2 tablespoons of the butter. Sweat the shallots over medium heat for 10 minutes, or until translucent. Add the sugar, vinegar, and lettuce to the pan and cook for 10 to 12 minutes, or until the lettuce is wilted. Add the Chicken Stock and simmer for 10 minutes. Add the pearl onions and radishes to the soup. Whisk in the remaining 3 1/2 tablespoons butter and season to taste with salt and pepper.

To prepare the foie gras: Season the foie gras cubes with salt and pepper. Cook the foie gras in a hot sauté pan over medium-high heat, turning to cook on all sides, for 1 1/2 minutes, or until just cooked. Reserve the cooked foie gras and foie gras fat.

ASSEMBLY Spoon some of the soup into each shallow bowl. Arrange the foie gras in the center of the soup. Drizzle the Herb Oil around the soup, sprinkle with the chives, and top with freshly ground black pepper.

Substitutions

Duck liver, chicken liver, tofu

Wine Notes

The sour element in the soup, powered by vinegar, provides the wine-pairing challenge in this dish. A dry style of German Riesling rises to the occasion. Zeltinger Schlossberg Riesling Kabinett made by Selbach-Oster from grapes grown on the steep, slatey slopes of the Mosel River, has a definitive racy acidity delicately balanced with elegant fruit. It cuts through the richness of the foie gras while taming the acidity of the vinegar.

Quail Breast with Peppered-Pistachio Crust, Pulped Heirloom Tomato, and Eggplant Purée

This preparation has robust flavor notes evocative of the Mediterranean. The pistachios carry a sweetness that is cut by the black pepper, while a rich, satiny eggplant purée is tamed by the tomato element. The quail meat itself is just sturdy enough to stand up to these simultaneously assertive and mellow flavors.

Serves 4

1 shallot, minced

2 cloves garlic, minced

5 tablespoons olive oil

5 Yellow Taxi tomatoes, peeled, seeded, and diced

1 teaspoon fennel seeds, toasted and coarsely ground

1/2 teaspoon cumin seeds, toasted and coarsely ground

1/4 teaspoon ground cayenne pepper

5 tablespoons water

Salt and pepper

1 teaspoon chopped fresh tarragon

2 small white eggplants

1/2 cup sugar

1/2 cup chopped pistachios

1 teaspoon pepper

3 tablespoons chopped dried black currants

8 quail breasts, frenched

2 tablespoons grapeseed oil

1/2 cup loosely packed fenugreek sprouts (or sunflower sprouts)

METHOD To prepare the chutney: Sweat the shallot and garlic in 1 tablespoon of the olive oil in a medium saucepan over medium heat for 1 minute. Add the yellow tomatoes, fennel seeds, cumin, and cayenne and cook over medium-low heat, stirring occasionally, for 30 minutes. Add 2 tablespoons of the water and season with salt and pepper. Press one-third of the chutney through a fine-mesh sieve, reserving the juices that are passed and discarding the solids. Fold the tarragon into the tomato juices.

To prepare the eggplants: Preheat the oven to 350 degrees. Cut the eggplants in half and score the meat. Season with salt and pepper and rub with 1 tablespoon of the olive oil. Place cut side down in an ovenproof pan and add water to a depth of 1/4 inch. Roast in the oven for 45 minutes, or until tender. Cool slightly and scrape the meat from the skin. Purée with the remaining olive oil (additional water may be necessary to form a smooth purée). Pass through a fine-mesh sieve and season to taste with salt and pepper.

To prepare the quails: Place the sugar in a small sauté pan with the remaining 3 tablespoons water and gently swirl the sugar and water together, but do not stir. Melt the sugar over medium heat for 10 minutes, or until golden brown. Fold in the pistachios and 1 teaspoon pepper and remove from the heat. Pour onto a silpat-lined sheet pan and cool completely. Coarsely chop the praline and fold in the currants.

Season the quail breasts with salt and pepper and place in a hot sauté pan with the grapeseed oil. Cook over medium-high heat for 2 minutes on each side, or until just cooked. Crust the skin side of the quail breasts with some of the pistachio praline. Store the remainder in an airtight container.

ASSEMBLY Spoon some of the chutney in the center of each plate and arrange 2 quail breasts over the chutney. Spoon the eggplant purée and reserved tomato juices around the plate. Sprinkle the fenugreek sprouts around the plate and top with freshly ground black pepper.

Substitutions

Chicken, pork, partridge

Wine Notes

The many spicy elements here are somewhat tempered by the sweet nut praline and the rich roasted eggplant. To diminish the heat of the curry and black pepper further, a Spätlese-level Riesling is in order. Nackenheimer Rothenberg from Gunderloch, in the Rheinhessen, cleanses the palate and refreshes with a delicate sweetness and bright acidity.

Tea-Smoked Amish Chicken with Arugula Salad and Water Chestnut–Pancetta Vinaigrette

The clean, light flavors of this dish offer an invigorating combination of elements resulting in a preparation that is both soul satisfying and provocative. The tea flavor of the chicken breast adds a haunting flavor and further accentuates its smokiness. It also nicely complements the pancetta element. Water chestnuts, lychee pieces, and arugula perfectly offset the playfully smoky meat and the pancetta with distinctive, refreshing notes. A yogurt-based sauce rounds out this preparation with just the right creaminess.

Serves 4

1 cup rice vinegar

1 cup water

2 tablespoons kosher salt

2 tablespoons sugar

1 tablespoon grated lemon zest

2 whole cloves

1 teaspoon mustard seeds

1 teaspoon peppercorns

1 bay leaf

1/4 cup Darjeeling tea leaves

2 Amish chicken breasts, boned and skinned

3 cups hickory wood chips, soaked in water for 1 hour

Salt and pepper

4 ounces pancetta, cut into lardons

1 1/2 tablespoons apple cider vinegar

4 fresh water chestnuts, parboiled, peeled, and cut into brunoise

4 cups loosely packed baby arugula

6 lychee nuts, peeled, pitted, and cut into wedges

1/4 cup finely chopped Walnut Praline (recipe follows)

1/2 cup sheep's milk maple yogurt

1/4 cup loosely packed micro curly peppercress

1 horned melon, pulp from seeds reserved

METHOD To prepare the chicken: Place the rice vinegar, water, kosher salt, sugar, lemon zest, cloves, mustard seeds, peppercorns, and bay leaf in a medium saucepan. Bring to a simmer over medium heat and add the tea. Remove from the heat and steep for 3 minutes. Strain through a fine-mesh sieve and cool to room temperature. Place the chicken breasts in a shallow container and pour the cooled brine over the chicken. Cover with plastic wrap and refrigerate overnight.

Remove the chicken from the liquid and pat dry. Place in a smoker or a covered grill with the hickory chips and slowly smoke over medium-low heat for 20 to 30 minutes, or until cooked. Cool the chicken to room temperature. Thinly slice just prior to serving and season to taste with salt and pepper.

To prepare the vinaigrette: Cook the pancetta in a small sauté pan over medium heat for 5 minutes, or until crispy. Reserve the fat and the pancetta separately. Place the fat in a bowl and whisk in the apple cider vinegar and water chestnuts. Season to taste with salt and pepper. Warm the vinaigrette just prior to serving.

ASSEMBLY Toss the arugula with some of the warmed vinaigrette, season to taste with salt and pepper, and place in the center of each plate. Lay the chicken on top of the arugula and place the lychee nuts around the arugula. Spoon the remaining vinaigrette around the plate. Fold the Walnut Praline into the yogurt and spoon the mixture around the plate. Sprinkle the crispy pancetta and curly peppercress around the arugula. Drizzle the horned melon pulp around the plate and top with freshly ground black pepper.

Walnut Praline

Yield: 1/2 cup

1/4 cup sugar

2 tablespoons water

1/4 cup walnut pieces

METHOD Combine the sugar and water in a small, heavy-bottomed sauté pan and cook over medium heat for 10 minutes, or until golden brown. Swirl the pan as necessary to distribute the caramel. Stir in the nuts. If any of the sugar crystallizes, continue to cook over low heat to melt. Pour onto a silpat-lined or lightly oiled nonstick sheet pan. Let cool and chop coarsely. Store in an airtight container at room temperature until ready to use.

Substitutions

Smoked ham, pork, pheasant, shrimp

Wine Notes

A spicy Riesling with good acidity is the match for the peppery arugula and peppercress and the smoky flavors from the chicken and pancetta. Niersteiner Paterberg Riesling Kabinett from Strub in the Rheinhessen in Germany is a style that has a definite raciness typical to the appellation and elegant fruit that also picks up on the lychee and horned melon elements.

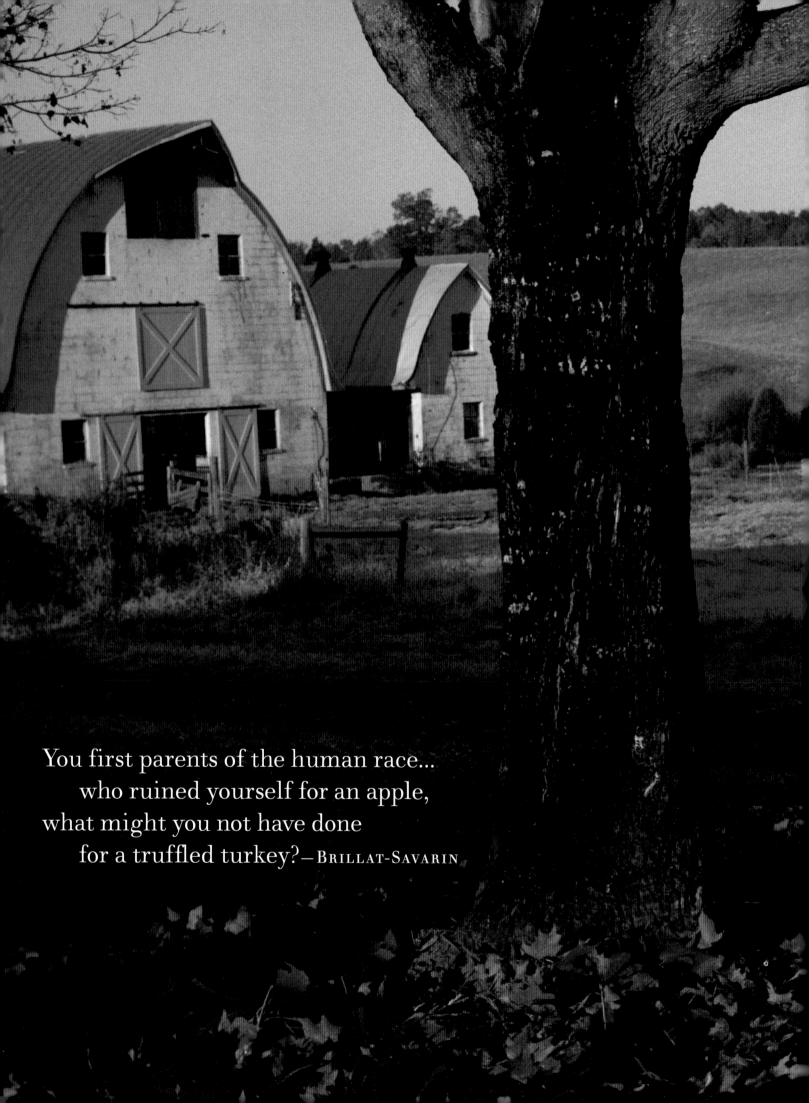

You first parents of the human race...
who ruined yourself for an apple,
what might you not have done
for a truffled turkey? —BRILLAT-SAVARIN

KODAK PMZ 6216 50

Poussin with Sweet-and-Sour Cardoon, Asparagus, Fava Beans, Opal Basil Vinegar, and Olive Oil–Shallot Sabayon

Here, poussin breasts are paired with one of my favorite vegetables, cardoon.
Its assertive yet delicately bitter-and-sweet flavor, with notes of artichoke and celery,
is an ideal match for the clean, light taste of the poussin. Fava beans add a pleasant earthy
starchiness, and white and green asparagus provide an elegant, just-crunchy texture.

Serves 4

1 cup white wine vinegar

1 cup red wine vinegar

1/4 cup plus 1 tablespoon sugar

2 cups firmly packed opal basil leaves

1 1/2 cups shelled fava beans, parboiled and peeled

1/3 cup ice water

1/4 cup plus 1/3 cup olive oil

1/4 cup firmly packed fresh flat-leaf parsley, blanched and shocked

1/4 cup firmly packed spinach, blanched and shocked

Salt and pepper

1/2 cup dry white wine

1 tablespoon plus 2 teaspoons minced shallot

2 egg yolks

1/2 teaspoon togarashi

1 teaspoon rice vinegar

1 cup water

2 stalks cardoon, peeled and sliced on the diagonal into fi-inch-thick pieces

6 large white asparagus spears, peeled and parboiled

1 tablespoon butter

12 yellow wax beans, parboiled and finely cut on the diagonal

2 tablespoons capers, rinsed

12 2-inch-long green asparagus tips, parboiled

2 teaspoons minced fresh basil

2 teaspoons minced fresh flat-leaf parsley

4 poussin breasts, boned

2 teaspoons grapeseed oil

1 tablespoon micro opal basil

1 tablespoon micro radish sprouts

METHOD To prepare the opal basil vinegar: Place the white and red wine vinegars in a saucepan with 1/4 cup of the sugar. Simmer over medium heat for 15 minutes, or until reduced to 1 cup. Cool slightly and purée with the opal basil until smooth. Refrigerate for 2 hours. Strain through a fine-mesh sieve and warm just prior to serving.

To prepare the fava bean purée: Purée 1/2 cup of the fava beans, the ice water, 2 tablespoons of the olive oil, the blanched parsley, and the spinach until smooth. Pass through a fine-mesh sieve and season with salt and pepper. Warm just prior to serving. Warm the remaining fava beans in a separate saucepan just prior to serving.

To prepare the sabayon: Place the white wine and 2 teaspoons of the shallot in a small saucepan and cook over medium heat until the wine just coats the bottom of the pan. Remove from the heat, add 1/3 cup of the olive oil and the egg yolks, and whisk the mixture together. Return the pan to the stove and cook over very low heat, whisking constantly, until the mixture has a ribbon-like consistency. Remove from the heat and season to taste with salt and pepper.

To prepare the cardoon: Place the togarashi, the remaining 1 tablespoon sugar, the rice vinegar, and 1/2 cup of the water in a sauté pan and simmer over medium heat for 1 minute, or until the sugar is dissolved. Add the cardoon and cook for 5 minutes, or until tender. Season with salt and pepper.

To prepare the white asparagus purée: Chop the white asparagus and purée with the remaining 1/2 cup water until smooth. Warm the purée in a small saucepan, whisk in the butter, and season with salt and pepper.

To prepare the yellow wax beans: Sweat the remaining 1 tablespoon shallot in the remaining 2 tablespoons olive oil in a sauté pan over medium heat for 30 seconds. Add the yellow wax beans, capers, and green asparagus tips and cook for 3 minutes, or until hot. Add the minced basil and parsley and season to taste with salt and pepper.

To prepare the poussin breasts: Season the breasts with salt and pepper. Place in a hot sauté pan with the grapeseed oil and cook for 5 to 7 minutes on each side, or until just cooked. Slice each breast in half and season to taste with salt and pepper.

ASSEMBLY Arrange some of the warm fava beans and cardoon in the center of each plate. Place 2 halves of the poussin over the vegetables. Spoon the sabayon, white asparagus purée, fava bean sauce, and opal basil vinegar around the plate. Spoon the wax bean mixture over the poussin, and sprinkle the micro opal basil and micro radish sprouts around the plates. Top with pepper.

Substitutions

Chicken, pork, salmon

Wine Notes

The prominent flavors in this dish—spicy togarashi, sweet-and-sour cardoon, opal basil vinegar—are well balanced by the acidity of Sauvignon Blanc from California. *Musque* from Cain is a style from Monterey that adds an aromatic floral component to the dish. Bigger styles with minimal to no oak will also work, such as Duckhorn's Sauvignon Blanc from Napa Valley.

Quail Stuffed with Wild Rice, Water Chestnuts, and Apple with Apple Cider Vinegar Emulsion

The delicately plump and succulent quail literally floats on the apple-flavored sweet-and-sour froth. Earthy, toothsome wild rice and apple pieces are kept moist within the cavity of the bird, and water chestnuts add a pleasing crispness. This dish is easy to prepare, and although it has a slight rusticity, it is quite light.

Serves 4

2 cups cooked wild rice

1/2 cup parboiled, peeled, medium-diced fresh water chestnuts

1 cup medium-diced red apple, skin on

Salt and pepper

4 whole quails

1 tablespoon grapeseed oil

1 tablespoon chopped fresh tarragon

1 tablespoon chopped fresh flat-leaf parsley

1/4 cup butter, melted

2 shallots, minced

1/4 cup plus 2 tablespoons butter

1 cup fresh apple cider

2 red apples, peeled and chopped

1/3 cup apple cider vinegar

6 sprigs fresh thyme

1 1/2 cups Chicken Stock (see Appendices)

1 small Fuji apple, skin on, cut into large dice

2 tablespoons chopped fresh chervil

METHOD To prepare the quails: Preheat the oven to 400 degrees. Toss the wild rice, water chestnuts, and medium-diced apple together in a bowl and season to taste with salt and pepper. Season the inside cavity and the outside of each quail with salt and pepper. Place half of the stuffing inside the birds and truss with butcher's twine. Reserve the remaining wild rice mixture.

Sear the quails with the grapeseed oil in a hot sauté pan over medium-high heat for 2 minutes on each side. Combine the tarragon, parsley, and melted butter in a small bowl. Transfer the quail to a roasting pan and baste with the melted butter mixture. Roast in the oven, basting occasionally, for 20 minutes, or until done. Remove the butcher's twine.

To prepare the apple cider emulsion: Sweat the shallots in a small saucepan over medium heat with 1 tablespoon of the butter for 5 minutes, or until translucent. Add the apple cider and cook for 5 minutes, or until reduced to 1/2 cup. Add the chopped apple and cook for 4 minutes. Add the apple cider vinegar and cook for 2 minutes. Add the thyme sprigs and Chicken Stock and simmer for 10 minutes. Strain through a fine-mesh sieve and season to taste with salt and pepper. Whisk in the remaining 1/4 cup butter and froth using a handheld blender just prior to serving.

To prepare the apple: Sauté the Fuji apple in the remaining 1 tablespoon butter in a small sauté pan over medium heat for 5 minutes, or until caramelized.

ASSEMBLY Spoon the remaining wild rice mixture in the center of each shallow bowl. Place a quail over the rice. Arrange some of the sautéed apple around the quail and spoon the apple cider emulsion in the bowl. Sprinkle the chervil around the bowls and top with freshly ground black pepper.

Substitutions

Poussin, game hen, chicken, scallops

Wine Notes

The apple contributes a crisp, zesty tang to this dish, and the wild rice emanates subtle anise and brown clove spice notes. A bit richer than Alsatian Pinot Blanc, though with lower acidity and displaying a nice spiced character, Pinot Auxerrois, well crafted by a wine maker like Jean Meyer of JosMeyer in Colmar, is a wine that adds yet another appealing layer of flavor to the delicately textured quail.

Muscovy Duck Salad with Black Truffle, Pont l'Évêque, Currants, and Port Reduction

This salad of just-warm duck breast and Perigord black truffle is pushed over the top with the addition of meltingly soft Pont l'Évêque slices sitting on crispy fruit-nut bread croutons. Walnuts add an additional crunchiness, and dried currants and a Port Reduction provide sweet fruit notes that help cut the richness of the meat. A twist of pepper is all that is required to finish this sure-to-satisfy combination of flavors and textures.

Serves 4

¹/₃ cup dried black currants

¹/₂ cup Port Reduction (see Appendices)

1 black truffle, thinly sliced

3 tablespoons olive oil

Salt and pepper

2 medium Muscovy duck breasts, boned and skin scored

2 teaspoons grapeseed oil

1 cup firmly packed tiny lettuces (such as frisée, baby red cress, and mâche)

2 teaspoons sherry wine vinegar

8 small slices Pont l'Évêque cheese, at room temperature

8 1¹/₂ by 1-inch slices fruit-nut bread, toasted

4 teaspoons walnut oil

¹/₄ cup toasted, chopped walnuts

METHOD To prepare the currants: Place the currants and Port Reduction in a small saucepan over medium heat and bring to a simmer. Keep warm until ready to use.

To prepare the truffle: Place the truffle slices and 1 tablespoon of the olive oil in a small saucepan over low heat for 2 to 3 minutes, or until warm. Season to taste with salt.

To prepare the duck: Season the duck breasts with salt and pepper. Place the duck, skin side down, in a hot sauté pan with the grapeseed oil and cook over medium-high heat for 4 to 5 minutes, or until the skin is golden brown and crispy. Turn over the duck and cook for 3 minutes, or until medium. Allow the duck to rest for 2 minutes, then thinly slice each breast. Season to taste with salt and pepper.

To prepare the greens: Toss the greens with the remaining 2 tablespoons olive oil and the sherry wine vinegar and season to taste with salt and pepper.

ASSEMBLY Place 1 slice of the cheese on each piece of the fruit-nut bread and arrange 2 pieces in the center of each plate. Arrange some of the truffle slices in front of the croutons, and place 3 slices of the duck leaning upright against the croutons. Arrange some of the greens on top of the duck and around the plate. Spoon the currants and Port Reduction around the plate. Drizzle the walnut oil and any juices from the truffles around the plate. Sprinkle with the walnuts and top with freshly ground black pepper.

Substitutions

Chicken, beef, pork, squab

Wine Notes

Crisp-skinned duck and crunchy walnuts provide the textural contrast to the creamy Pont l'Évêque, which demands a wine with acidity and some sweetness. This is a fun salad that evokes the desire for spicy, aromatic Alsatian varietals. *Rangen de Thann*, grand cru Tokay Pinot Gris from Domaine Zind-Humbrecht, has a big extracted style that is delicious with the cheese and is not overwhelmed by the duck or Port Reduction.

Pheasant Salad with Foie Gras, Matsutake Mushrooms, Tamarind, Asian Pear, and Hazelnut Vinaigrette

This type of salad has many possible variations in ingredients: different meats, nuts, fruits, and lettuces. Here, delicate pheasant breast and buttery lettuces are paired with rich hazelnuts and foie gras. These are pushed into balance with sweet Asian pear pieces and with the elegant astringency of tamarind. Crispy apple chips, tiny croutons, and a poached quail egg add depth and complexity.

Serves 4

1 large pheasant breast, boned and skin removed and reserved

1/2 cup plus 1 teaspoon grapeseed oil

Salt and pepper

1/4 cup freshly squeezed orange juice

1/4 cup tamarind paste

1 teaspoon minced shallot

3 tablespoons sherry wine vinegar

1/4 cup hazelnut oil

4 1-ounce portions foie gras, cleaned

2 cups loosely packed baby lettuces (such as red oak and mâche)

2 tablespoons toasted, skinned, and quartered hazelnuts

1/2 cup Asian pear batons

3 matsutake mushrooms, cleaned and thinly sliced

1 small head Belgian endive, cored and cut into 1/8-inch-thick rings

1 Pickled Lamb Tongue, cut into 4 slices (see Appendices)

4 quail eggs, soft poached

1/2 cup small-diced brioche, toasted

4 Oven-Dried Apple Chips (see Appendices)

METHOD To prepare the cracklings: Cut the pheasant skin into 1/4-inch-wide strips. Place the skin and 1/4 cup of the grapeseed oil in a small saucepan over medium-low heat and slowly render the fat for 20 minutes, or until the skin is golden brown and crispy. Remove the crisp skin from the oil and blot on paper towels. Season to taste with salt and pepper. Discard the fat.

To prepare the tamarind: Place the orange juice and tamarind paste in a small saucepan. Cook over medium-low heat for 5 minutes, or until just warm. Whisk together until smooth and season to taste with salt and pepper.

To prepare the vinaigrette: Place the shallot and sherry wine vinegar in a small bowl. Slowly whisk in the hazelnut oil and 1/4 cup of the grapeseed oil and season to taste with salt and pepper.

To prepare the pheasant breast: Season the pheasant breast with salt and pepper. Place the breast in a hot sauté pan with the remaining 1 teaspoon grapeseed oil and cook over medium heat for 5 minutes on each side, or until golden brown and just cooked. Let rest for 3 minutes, then thinly slice the breast and season to taste with salt and pepper.

To prepare the foie gras: Season the foie gras with salt and pepper. Place the foie gras in a hot sauté pan and cook over medium-high heat for 1 minute on each side, or until cooked medium-rare.

To prepare the salad: Place the lettuces, hazelnuts, Asian pear, mushrooms, and endive in a medium bowl. Gently toss the ingredients together. Lightly coat the salad with some of the vinaigrette and season to taste with salt and pepper.

ASSEMBLY Spoon the tamarind purée in 3 lines in the center of each plate. Place some of the salad mixture over the tamarind purée. Lay a slice of lamb tongue, a piece of foie gras, and a few pheasant slices over the salad. Arrange more of the salad mixture over the lamb tongue. Place a soft-poached quail egg on the outer portion of the salad. Sprinkle the toasted brioche croutons and cracklings around the plate, and drizzle some of the hazelnut vinaigrette around the salad. Place an Oven-Dried Apple Chip in the center of the salad and top with freshly ground black pepper.

Substitutions

Chicken, scallops, pork

Wine Notes

The assertive sweet and smoky notes from the Pickled Lamb Tongue are well matched by Vendange Tardive Tokay Pinot Gris from the Alsace. *Altenberg*, a grand cru wine from Albert Mann, pulls together the sweet, sour, and smoky elements. At the same time, it cuts through the richness of the foie gras and provides an interesting mineral note. Domaine Zind-Humbrecht produces a Tokay Pinot Gris, *Vieilles Vignes*, with a similar profile.

Chicken Breast with Peaches, Tatsoi, and Marjoram

This light preparation makes an ideal first course for something more substantial.
Although it comes across as a salad, the dish certainly can be served as a meal in itself.
Braised legumes, or even something more toothsome like soba noodles, can be added
to provide more substance. Figs would be a fine substitute for the peaches.

Serves 4

2 peaches, peeled and pitted

2 teaspoons freshly squeezed lemon juice

1½ cups freshly squeezed orange juice

2 chicken breasts, boned

Salt and pepper

2 teaspoons fresh thyme leaves

4 teaspoons grapeseed oil

1½ cups loosely packed baby tatsoi

3 teaspoons olive oil

1 white peach, skin on, pitted and cut into 20 wedges

4 teaspoons chopped fresh marjoram

METHOD To prepare the dried peaches: Preheat the oven to 225 degrees. Slice the peeled peaches into ¼-inch-thick slices and place on a wire rack–lined sheet pan. Lightly coat the peach slices with the lemon juice. Dry the peaches in the oven for 2 hours, or until dry to the touch.

Remove the peaches from the oven and cut into batons.

To prepare the orange juice reduction: Place the orange juice in a small saucepan and simmer over medium-low heat for 20 minutes, or until reduced to ½ cup.

To prepare the chicken: Season the chicken breasts with salt and pepper and sprinkle with the thyme leaves. Cook the breasts, skin side down first, with the grapeseed oil in a hot sauté pan over medium-high heat for 3 to 4 minutes on each side, or until cooked. Let rest for 3 minutes, then slice each breast in half. Season to taste with salt and pepper.

ASSEMBLY Toss the tatsoi with 1 teaspoon of the olive oil and season to taste with salt and pepper. Arrange some of the tatsoi in the center of each plate. Place a piece of the chicken over the tatsoi allowing some of the tatsoi to show through the top and bottom of the chicken breast. Arrange 5 fresh peach wedges and 5 dried peach slices in a fan at the top of the chicken breast. Spoon the orange juice reduction around the plate and drizzle with the remaining 2 teaspoons olive oil. Sprinkle the marjoram over the chicken and around the plate. Top with freshly ground black pepper.

Substitutions

Pork, turkey, pheasant

Wine Notes

An Alsatian Tokay Pinot Gris has the ability to harmonize the herbal green elements, peppery tatsoi, and the sweet orange juice and peaches. An off-dry style in most vintages, Domaine Zind-Humbrecht's spicy *Rangen de Thann* will stand up and be noticed.

Muscovy Duck Breast with Ginger-Soy-Hijiki Broth, Water Chestnuts, and Preserved Pineapple

The flavors of this soul-satisfying dish are striking and complex, but at the same time the whole thing comes across as light and clean. The preserved pineapple cuts perfectly into the lucsious duck meat, delivering just the right balance of sweet and sour. The broth, flavored with ginger, soy, hijiki seaweed, and garlic is simultaneously assertive yet refined. Rice or noodles could easily be added, making the preparation a meal in itself.

Serves 4

¼ cup thinly sliced pineapple

½ cup Pickling Juice (see Appendices)

⅛ teaspoon celery seeds

¼ teaspoon ground Szechuan peppercorns

½ teaspoon finely chopped fresh flat-leaf parsley

1 teaspoon finely chopped lemon zest

2 Muscovy duck breasts, boned, skin scored, and excess fat trimmed

Salt and pepper

2 teaspoons grapeseed oil

2 cups loosely packed tatsoi leaves

4 fresh water chestnuts, boiled, peeled, and thinly sliced

2 tablespoons dried hijiki seaweed, soaked in water overnight and drained

Ginger-Soy-Hijiki Broth (recipe follows)

4 teaspoons sesame oil

2 tablespoons micro tatsoi sprouts

METHOD To prepare the pineapple: Place the pineapple in the Pickling Juice and refrigerate for 1 hour. Place the mixture in a small saucepan and warm over medium heat for 3 minutes, or until hot. Drain the pineapple just prior to serving.

To prepare the spice mixture: Toast the celery seeds and Szechuan peppercorns in a small sauté pan over medium heat for 1½ minutes. Remove from the heat, pour into a small bowl, and toss with the parsley and lemon zest.

To prepare the duck: Season the duck breasts with salt and pepper. Place them, skin side down, in a hot sauté pan with the grapeseed oil and cook over medium heat for 6 to 7 minutes on each side, or until the skin is crispy and the meat is cooked medium-rare. Let rest for 3 minutes, then cut into ¼-inch-thick slices. Season to taste with salt and the spice mixture.

ASSEMBLY Place some of the tatsoi leaves, water chestnuts, pineapple, and hijiki seaweed in the center of each shallow bowl. Arrange the duck breast slices in a pinwheel on top and pour the hot broth into the bowl. Sprinkle any remaining spice mixture over the duck, drizzle the sesame oil around the bowl, and sprinkle with the tatsoi sprouts.

Ginger-Soy-Hijiki Broth

Yield: 1 quart

½ cup dried hijiki seaweed

½ cup water

2 tablespoons finely diced jalapeño chile

2 shallots, finely diced

½ cup minced fresh ginger

1 tablespoon minced garlic

1 tablespoon sesame oil

½ cup plus 1 tablespoon rice vinegar

¾ cup mirin

1¼ cups plus 2 tablespoons tamari soy sauce

3 cups Chicken Stock (see Appendices)

Salt and pepper

METHOD Soak the hijiki in the water for 30 minutes and drain. Sauté the jalapeño, shallots, ginger, and garlic with the sesame oil in a medium saucepan over medium heat for 1 minute. Add the rice vinegar, mirin, tamari, hijiki, and Chicken Stock and bring to a simmer. Season to taste with salt and pepper.

Substitutions

Squab, chicken, salmon, bass

Wine Notes

The delicious salty Asian broth and pickled pineapple flavors are assertive in this dish and dominate the palate. A spicy, low-acid white will match these high-toned notes. Gewürztraminer *Cuvée Laurence* from Domaine Weinbach is a high-extract white with lower residual sugar that matches the ginger spice and fruit notes without feeling cloying.

Terrine of Chicken Breast and Lobster with Salsify—Chicken Liver "Napoleon" and Salsify Vinaigrette

*Lobster and chicken work well together, and here they are layered to form
a succulent terrine. Next to the terrine, for a whimsical note, is a "napoleon" made from
Crispy Potato Tuiles, salsify, and peppery watercress. These two components
consumed together provide contrasting and complementary flavors and textures.
A shellfish vinaigrette adds richness and acid and smoothly finishes the dish.*

Serves 16

1 quart Shellfish Stock (see Appendices)

4 sheets gelatin

4 chicken breasts, boned and skinned

Salt and pepper

4 cups Chicken Stock (see Appendices)

4 sprigs thyme

4 sprigs flat-leaf parsley

8 small lobster tails, steamed and shells removed

3 cups loosely packed watercress sprigs, stems removed

1 cup Port

1 pound chicken livers, cleaned

1 cup butter

4 tablespoons minced shallot

1 Granny Smith apple, peeled and diced

1/4 orange, peeled

1/3 cup brandy

2 cups Pickling Juice (see Appendices)

2 stalks salsify, peeled and thinly sliced on the diagonal

4 cups freshly squeezed orange juice

10 teaspoons Shellfish Oil (see Appendices)

Fleur de sel

1/2 cup peeled, julienned Granny Smith apple

32 Crispy Potato Tuiles (recipe follows)

4 teaspoons fresh lemon verbena chiffonade

METHOD To prepare the aspic: Cook the Shellfish Stock in a medium saucepan over medium heat for 1 hour, or until reduced to 1 cup. Bloom the gelatin in a bowl of cold water for 5 minutes. Remove the gelatin from the water and add it to the warm Shellfish Stock. Simmer the mixture over medium-low heat for 2 minutes, or until the gelatin is dissolved.

To prepare the chicken: Season the chicken breasts with salt and pepper. Place the breasts, Chicken Stock, thyme, and parsley in a saucepan. Bring the mixture to a very slow simmer and poach the chicken breasts over low heat for 10 to 13 minutes, or until the chicken is just cooked. Remove the chicken from the poaching liquid and cool completely. Cut the chicken breasts lengthwise into 1½-inch-wide pieces and square off the ends. Cut the chicken breast strips into ¼-inch-thick pieces and season to taste with salt and pepper.

To prepare the lobster: Trim the edges of the lobster tails to form 1½-inch-wide pieces with squared-off ends. Cut the lobster pieces into ¼-inch-thick slices and season to taste with salt and pepper.

To assemble the terrine: Line an 8 by 1½ by 2¼-inch terrine mold with plastic wrap, allowing some to drape over the sides. Place a layer of the lobster on the bottom of the terrine mold with the red side facing down. Brush the lobster with some of the aspic and place a layer of the chicken over the lobster. Brush the chicken with the aspic and cover with a layer of the watercress sprigs. Brush the watercress with the aspic and continue the process by layering the lobster, chicken, watercress, lobster, chicken, and a final layer of lobster, brushing each layer with the aspic. (You will have watercress left over.) Firmly press down on the terrine with your fingers or a small wooden board. Fold the excess plastic wrap over the terrine and refrigerate for 3 hours, or until set. (The terrine can be assembled the day before and refrigerated overnight.)

Remove the terrine from the mold and rewrap tightly in plastic wrap. With the plastic wrap on, cut the terrine into ½-inch-thick slices. Carefully remove the plastic wrap from the terrine slices and season the slices to taste with salt and pepper.

To prepare the mousse: Place the Port in a small saucepan and bring to a simmer. Cook the Port over low heat for 30 minutes, or until reduced to ¼ cup. Season the livers with salt and pepper. Place the livers in a hot sauté pan with the butter and shallot and sear over medium-high heat for 1 minute on each side. Add the diced apple, orange, and brandy and cook for 5 minutes, or until the brandy has been absorbed. Add the reduced Port and purée the mixture until smooth. Pass through a fine-mesh sieve and season to taste with salt and pepper. Refrigerate the mousse for 2 hours, or until set.

To prepare the salsify: Warm the Pickling Juice in a small saucepan. Add the salsify and simmer over medium-low heat for 5 minutes, or until tender. Cool in the liquid.

To prepare the vinaigrette: Place the orange juice in a medium saucepan and simmer over medium heat for 45 minutes, or until reduced to ½ cup. Whisk in the Shellfish Oil and season to taste with salt and pepper.

ASSEMBLY Place a slice of terrine on an angle toward the bottom of each plate and sprinkle with fleur de sel. Place a spoonful of the chicken liver mousse 1½ inches to the right of the terrine. Toss the remaining watercress with 1½ tablespoons of the vinaigrette and season to taste with salt and

continued on page 233

Dairyless Celery Root Soup with Chicken Livers, Roasted Tiny Granny Smith Apples, and Thyme

The luscious pieces of liver and the sweet roasted apple rings soar with flavor against the backdrop of the clean, elegant celery root soup. In total, the soup features extraordinary textures and flavors flawlessly melting together. Notes of thyme and Thyme Oil are the only accents needed.

Serves 4

½ cup slab bacon batons

12 sprigs thyme

3 cups chopped celery root

2 quarts Vegetable Stock (see Appendices)

Salt and pepper

4 tiny Granny Smith apples, peeled and sliced into ¼-inch-thick rings

¼ cup butter, melted

⅓ cup plus ½ teaspoon apple cider vinegar

1 cup celery root batons

2 tablespoons butter

4 chicken livers, cleaned

2 tablespoons grapeseed oil

4 teaspoons fresh thyme leaves

4 teaspoons Thyme Oil (recipe follows)

METHOD To prepare the soup: Cook the bacon in a medium saucepan over medium heat for 4 minutes, or until the fat is rendered from the bacon. Add 8 of the thyme sprigs, the chopped celery root, and the Vegetable Stock and simmer over medium heat for 15 to 20 minutes, or until the celery root is tender. Remove and discard the thyme sprigs and purée the soup until smooth. Strain through a fine-mesh sieve and season to taste with salt and pepper. Reheat just prior to serving.

To prepare the apples: Preheat the oven to 400 degrees. Brush the apples with the melted butter and place in a roasting pan with the remaining 4 thyme sprigs and any extra melted butter. Roast in the oven for 20 minutes, or until the apples are caramelized and tender. Remove from the oven and stir in the apple cider vinegar to deglaze the pan.

To prepare the celery root: Sauté the celery root batons with 2 tablespoons butter in a hot sauté pan over medium-high heat for 2 to 3 minutes, or until golden brown and tender. Season to taste with salt and pepper.

To prepare the livers: Season the chicken livers with salt and pepper. Place the livers in a hot sauté pan with the grapeseed oil and cook for 1½ minutes on each side, or until cooked medium. Slice each liver into 4 pieces on the diagonal.

ASSEMBLY Ladle some of the soup into each shallow bowl. Arrange 3 apple slices and 4 pieces of the liver in each bowl. Place some of the celery root batons around the bowl. Sprinkle with the thyme leaves and drizzle the Thyme Oil around the bowl.

Thyme Oil

Yield: ½ cup

½ cup firmly packed fresh thyme leaves
1 cup firmly packed spinach
½ cup plus 1 tablespoon grapeseed oil
¼ cup olive oil

METHOD Sauté the thyme leaves and spinach with 1 tablespoon of the grapeseed oil in a small sauté pan over medium heat for 2 minutes, or until wilted. Immediately shock in ice water and drain. Coarsely chop the mixture and squeeze out the excess water. Purée the spinach mixture with the remaining ½ cup grapeseed oil and the olive oil for 3 to 4 minutes, or until bright green. Pour into a container, cover, and refrigerate for 1 day.

Strain the oil through a fine-mesh sieve and discard the solids. Refrigerate for 1 day, decant, and refrigerate until ready to use or up to 2 weeks.

Substitutions

Foie gras, squab liver, chicken

Wine Notes

The density of the creamy celery root and rich chicken livers are cut by the bright apple components and fresh thyme. A wine that is broad yet finishes crisp will fill out and enliven this dish. The Monterey Pinot Blanc from Chalone gains extra texture from sweet oak, but also finishes on a high note of bright acidity.

Chicken "Oysters" with a Ragout of Root Vegetables, Parsnip Purée, and Salsify–Black Truffle Vinaigrette

Although the components of this rustic combination are earthy, the result is an extremely regal and refined preparation. The tender nuggets from the back of the chicken are the perfect morsels to rest atop a bed of meltaway root vegetables. A parsnip purée provides a sating richness, while a truffled salsify vinaigrette adds just the right headiness. Notes of sage bring on mystery.

Serves 4

¹/₂ cup small peeled carrot wedges

¹/₂ cup small peeled turnip wedges

¹/₂ cup small peeled celery root wedges

¹/₂ cup small peeled parsnip wedges

1 tablespoon butter

Salt and pepper

¹/₂ cup peeled, chopped parsnip

1¹/₂ cups milk

1 stalk salsify, peeled and cut into 4 pieces

1 tablespoon sherry wine vinegar

¹/₂ cup olive oil

2 tablespoons brunoise-cut black truffle

12 chicken oysters

1 tablespoon grapeseed oil

¹/₄ cup Meat Stock Reduction, hot (see Appendices)

2 teaspoons chopped fresh sage

METHOD To prepare the root vegetables: Sauté the carrot, turnip, celery root, and parsnip wedges with the butter in a small saucepan over medium heat for 5 to 8 minutes, or until golden brown. Season to taste with salt and pepper.

To prepare the parsnip purée: Cook the chopped parsnip with fi cup of the milk in a small saucepan over medium-low heat for 10 minutes, or until tender. Purée the parsnip with enough of the milk to create a smooth sauce. Season with salt and pepper.

To prepare the salsify vinaigrette: Cook the salsify with the remaining 1 cup milk in a small saucepan over medium-low heat for 10 to 12 minutes, or until tender. Remove the salsify from the liquid and cut in half lengthwise, then into ¹/₈-inch-thick slices. Whisk together the sherry wine vinegar and olive oil in a small bowl. Fold in the salsify and black truffle and season to taste with salt and pepper.

To prepare the chicken oysters: Season the chicken oysters with salt and pepper. Sauté the chicken in a hot sauté pan with the grapeseed oil over medium-high heat for 2 minutes on each side, or until done.

ASSEMBLY Place 3 of the chicken oysters in the center of each plate and arrange some of the root vegetables around the chicken oysters. Spoon the salsify vinaigrette over and around the root vegetables. Spoon the parsnip purée in a ring around the outside of the root vegetables. Spoon the Meat Stock Reduction over the chicken oysters and around the plate and top with the sage and freshly ground black pepper.

Substitutions

Chicken breast, pork, duck, scallops

Wine Notes

A natural marriage exists between white Rhône varietals and root vegetables. Roussane-based Châteauneuf-du-Pape blancs from producers like Château de Beaucastel or Château Rayas have a ripe, mouth-filling fruit that complements the various vegetables without dominating the delicate, crispy chicken oysters.

Dairyless Garlic Soup with Smoked Poulard, Eggplant, Fennel Confit, and Fennel Emulsion

Although this dish is very lusty and earthy due to the sensual garlic purée and the luscious pieces of smoked poulard, it actually comes across as quite delicate because of the clean, light notes of the fennel. Eggplant provides a wonderful meaty texture note along with additional earthiness, and wisps of fennel sprouts deliver a final whimsical element.

Serves 4

36 cloves garlic

2 cups olive oil

6 sprigs thyme

2 cups Vegetable Stock (see Appendices)

Salt and pepper

1/4 cup plus 2 tablespoons butter

1 fennel bulb, finely chopped

*1 Granny Smith apple,
peeled and finely chopped*

1/4 cup water

*3 cups hickory wood chips,
soaked in water for 1 hour*

2 poulard breasts, boned and skinned

1 fennel bulb, chopped

*1/2 cup loosely packed fennel fronds,
blanched*

*1 Japanese eggplant, halved lengthwise
and sliced 1/4 inch thick*

2 teaspoons grapeseed oil

2 tablespoons micro fennel sprouts

1/4 teaspoon pink peppercorn flakes

METHOD To prepare the garlic soup: Place the garlic cloves in a saucepan and cover with the olive oil and thyme. Cook over low heat for 3 hours, or until very tender. Discard the thyme, and separately reserve 8 of the garlic cloves as garlic confit and 4 teaspoons of the cooking oil. Purée the remaining 28 cloves with the Vegetable Stock until smooth. Warm the soup in a medium saucepan over medium-low heat for 5 minutes, or until warm, and season to taste with salt and pepper.

To prepare the fennel confit: Place 2 tablespoons of the butter, the finely chopped fennel, and the apple in a sauté pan and cook for 10 minutes. Add the water and cook over medium-low heat for 1 hour, or until tender. Mash the fennel mixture with a fork and season to taste with salt and pepper.

To prepare the poulard: Drain the water from the wood chips. Season the poulard breasts with salt and pepper and place in a smoker or a covered grill with the hickory wood chips. Smoke the poulard breasts over medium-low heat for 40 minutes, or until cooked. Slice the breasts into 3/4-inch-thick pieces and season to taste with salt and pepper.

To prepare the fennel emulsion: Place the chopped fennel in a saucepan and cover with water. Cook the fennel over medium heat for 30 minutes. Reserve 1/2 cup of the fennel and all of the liquid. Purée the reserved fennel, the liquid, and the fennel fronds until smooth. Pass through a fine-mesh sieve and cook in a small saucepan over medium heat for 5 minutes, or until warm. Season to taste with salt and pepper and whisk in the remaining 1/4 cup butter. Froth with a handheld blender just prior to serving.

To prepare the eggplant: Place the eggplant in a hot sauté pan with the grapeseed oil and cook over medium heat for 3 to 5 minutes, or until tender. Season to taste with salt and pepper.

ASSEMBLY Spoon teaspoonfuls of the fennel confit at 5 spots in each shallow bowl. Arrange some of the eggplant and smoked poulard pieces around the bowl. Ladle in the warm garlic soup and place 2 pieces of the garlic confit in the bowl. Spoon the fennel emulsion and reserved 4 teaspoons garlic oil around the soup. Sprinkle with the fennel sprouts and pink peppercorn flakes.

Substitutions

Chicken, quail, pheasant

Wine Notes

The smoky, sweet flavors of the soup and poulard are cut nicely by the fennel and the crisp acidity from the apple. The white wines of St. Aubin extend the lush textural landscape of the dish. *En Charmois* from Marc Colin is a creamy Chardonnay that echoes the anise spice of the fennel.

Partridge in Its Consommé with Quinoa, Pom Pom Mushrooms, Caramelized Turnips, and Clove Oil

This preparation has fabulous earthy flavors but it is extremely light at the same time. The breast of partridge seemingly floats in the bed of quinoa, which is gorgeous with its nutty, straw-like aroma. Just-sautéed pom pom mushrooms provide an elegant earthiness with their extraordinarily delicate texture, and caramelized turnips add a playful bite. A rich note is provided by adding a soft-boiled quail egg. A few drops of Clove Oil are all that is needed in the Partridge Consommé to give this dish just the right exotic edge.

Serves 4

4 partridge breasts, boned

4 partridge legs

4 cinnamon sticks

8 whole cloves, toasted and crushed

1/2 cup olive oil

Salt and pepper

1 small turnip, peeled and cut into small wedges

3 tablespoons butter

2 pom pom mushrooms, cleaned and thinly sliced

1 1/2 cups cooked quinoa

2 tablespoons chopped fresh chives

4 quail eggs, soft boiled (about 3 minutes) and peeled

12 whole cloves

Partridge Consommé (see Appendices)

2 tablespoons diagonally cut 1-inch-long fresh chives

4 teaspoons Clove Oil (recipe follows)

METHOD To prepare the partridge: Toss the partridge breasts and legs in a large bowl with the cinnamon sticks, crushed cloves, and olive oil. Cover the bowl with plastic wrap and refrigerate overnight.

Remove the partridge pieces from the marinade and season with salt and pepper. Place the breasts, skin side down first, in a hot sauté pan over medium-high heat and cook for 3 minutes on each side, or until just cooked. Cook the leg meat for 5 minutes on each side, or until done. Remove the leg meat from the bone, cut into small dice, and reserve. Slice the partridge breasts in half on the diagonal just prior to serving.

To prepare the turnip: Place the turnip wedges in a hot sauté pan with 1 tablespoon of the butter and cook over medium-high heat for 3 to 4 minutes, or until caramelized. Season to taste with salt and pepper and keep warm.

To prepare the mushrooms: Place the mushrooms in a hot sauté pan with the remaining 2 tablespoons butter and cook over medium heat for 3 to 4 minutes, or until the mushrooms are tender and golden brown. Season to taste with salt and pepper and keep warm.

To prepare the quinoa: Warm the quinoa in a small saucepan over medium-low heat. Fold in the reserved leg meat and chopped chives and season with salt and pepper.

ASSEMBLY Spoon some of the quinoa mixture into the center of each bowl and top with a partridge breast. Arrange the mushrooms and caramelized turnips around the bowl. Gently break open the quail eggs and place 1 egg in each bowl. Sprinkle the whole cloves in the bowl and ladle in some of the hot consommé. Sprinkle the chives and drizzle the Clove Oil around the consommé.

Clove Oil

Yield: 1 cup

1 cup whole cloves

1/2 cup grapeseed oil

1/2 cup olive oil

METHOD Roast the cloves in a hot sauté pan over medium-high heat for 3 to 4 minutes, or until the aroma is very strong. Grind the cloves into a powder and place in a blender with the grapeseed and olive oils. Purée for 3 minutes, or until completely incorporated. Pour into a container and refrigerate for 48 hours. Strain the oil though a fine-mesh sieve and discard the solids. Refrigerate for 1 day, decant, and refrigerate until ready to use or for up to 2 weeks.

Substitutions

Quail, chicken, duck, pork

Wine Notes

Warmed by the hot consommé, the brown spice from the Clove Oil and cinnamon becomes a prominent aromatic component pervading this dish. The spice, earthy turnips, and nutty quinoa are set off nicely by a focused style of Puligny-Montrachet from Étienne Sauzet. His wines have a firm presence and a good acidity that finish nicely with the elegant broth.

Steamed Pheasant Breast with Hen of the Woods and Black Trumpet Mushrooms and Alba White Truffles

Steaming is among the most delicate ways to cook meats. The result is an ultrasucculent texture and a fully revealed flavor. Here, pheasant breast is first wrapped in leeks to help retain the juices, and then paired with earthy mushrooms and heady shavings of white truffle. The resulting mixture of textures and flavors is glorious.

Serves 4

40 tiny leeks (green portion only)

4 sprigs thyme

2 sprigs rosemary

2 cups dry white wine

2 bay leaves

1 teaspoon peppercorns

4 small pheasant breasts, boned and skinned

Salt and pepper

1 large Alba white truffle, shaved

1/4 cup plus 2 tablespoons butter, softened

8 teaspoons white truffle oil

2 teaspoons minced shallot

1 cup black trumpet mushrooms, cleaned and cut into small pieces

1 1/2 cups hen of the woods mushrooms, cleaned and separated

3 tablespoons Chicken Stock (see Appendices)

1/2 cup Pheasant Stock Reduction (see Appendices)

1 tablespoon chopped fresh flat-leaf parsley

4 pheasant livers, cleaned

2 teaspoons grapeseed oil

1/2 teaspoon fleur de sel

METHOD To prepare the leeks: Blanch the baby leek tops in boiling salted water for 1 minute. Shock in ice water and drain. Lay the leek tops on a flat surface and blot off any excess water. Carefully cut open the leeks and gently scrape the inside to remove any excess fibers. Lay a piece of plastic wrap on a flat surface. Lay 10 of the leek tops on the plastic wrap with the insides facing up and overlapping slightly. Cover with another piece of plastic and set aside. Repeat the process with the remaining leeks, creating 4 wraps in all.

To prepare the pheasant: Place the thyme, rosemary, white wine, bay leaves, and peppercorns in the bottom of a steamer. Season the pheasant breasts with salt and pepper and place in the prepared steamer. Bring the liquid to a simmer over medium-low heat, cover, and steam for 10 to 12 minutes, or until the pheasant is just cooked.

To prepare the white truffle butter: Coarsely chop one-fourth of the truffle shavings and fold into 1/4 cup of the butter. Stir in 4 teaspoons of the white truffle oil and season to taste with salt and pepper.

To assemble the pheasant: Remove the top layer of plastic from the prepared leek wraps. Carefully spread some of the white truffle butter over the leeks. Lay a pheasant breast in the center of each leek wrap and carefully wrap the pheasant breasts in the leeks, peeling back the plastic wrap as you go. Place the leek-wrapped pheasant breasts in the steamer and cook for 2 to 3 minutes, or until hot. Remove from the steamer and slice each pheasant breast in half crosswise.

To prepare the mushrooms: Sweat the shallot in the remaining 2 tablespoons butter in a medium saucepan over medium heat for 2 minutes, or until translucent. Add the mushrooms and Chicken Stock and cook for 3 to 4 minutes, or until the mushrooms are tender. Remove the mushrooms from the pan, add the Pheasant Stock Reduction and parsley, and season to taste with salt and pepper.

To prepare the livers: Season the livers with salt and pepper. Place the livers in a hot sauté pan with the grapeseed oil and cook over medium-high heat for 1 1/2 minutes on each side, or until cooked medium. Slice each liver in half.

ASSEMBLY Place 2 pheasant breast halves in the center of each plate. Place half of a liver on each side of the pheasant. Arrange the mushrooms around the plate. Spoon the mushroom cooking liquid and the remaining white truffle oil around the plate. Sprinkle the remaining shaved white truffles around the plate and sprinkle with the fleur de sel.

Substitutions

Chicken, hamachi, veal

Wine Notes

Redolent of heady white truffles and rich with meaty mushrooms, this dish can stand a Chardonnay with subtle oak influence. Puligny-Montrachet *La Truffière* from Jean-Marc Boillot is certainly an Old World–style Chardonnay, free of too-forward fruit or tropical flavors, instead displaying interesting layers of earth and mineral notes supported by a lush texture.

Quail with Fennel Sauce and Shaved Fennel

This preparation is light and simple and easily lends itself to a variety of possibilities.
The quail breasts sit on a little mound of shaved fennel that is flavored with lemon juice and pink peppercorns.
This mixture is not served warm so we have an enticing temperature contrast with the meat.
A fine purée of fennel along with basil and olive oils round out the dish, but it doesn't have to stop there.
Noodles could be added, or risotto, or even braised legumes. Or, greens could be introduced
and this could easily become a full-flavored salad.

Serves 4

1 large fennel bulb, chopped

5 cups water

2 cups loosely packed spinach, blanched and shocked

Salt and pepper

2 teaspoons pink peppercorn flakes

2 sprigs tarragon

1/4 cup dry white wine vinegar

2 teaspoons olive oil

1 1/2 cups shaved fennel

2 tablespoons freshly squeezed lemon juice

2 tablespoons chopped fennel fronds

8 quail breasts, frenched

1 tablespoon grapeseed oil

4 teaspoons Basil Oil (see Appendices)

METHOD To prepare the fennel sauce: Place the chopped fennel and water in a saucepan and simmer over medium-low heat for 1 hour. Strain the liquid and reserve ½ cup of the cooked fennel. Return the liquid to the saucepan and slowly simmer for 30 minutes, or until reduced to 2 cups. Purée the liquid with the spinach and the reserved fennel. Pass through a fine-mesh sieve and season to taste with salt and pepper. Warm just prior to serving.

To prepare the shaved fennel: Place the pink peppercorns, tarragon, and white wine vinegar in a small sauté pan. Cook over medium heat for 3 to 4 minutes, or until the vinegar just coats the bottom of the pan. Remove the tarragon and add the olive oil, shaved fennel, and lemon juice. Cook over medium heat for 5 minutes, or until warm. Season to taste with salt and pepper and fold in 1 tablespoon of the fennel fronds.

To prepare the quail: Season the quail breasts with salt and pepper. Place the breasts in a hot sauté pan with the grapeseed oil and cook for 2 minutes on each side, or until just cooked. Slice each quail breast in half on the diagonal and season to taste with salt and pepper.

ASSEMBLY Place some of the shaved fennel at the top of each plate. Place 2 quail breasts in the center of each plate. Spoon the fennel sauce around the plate and drizzle the Basil Oil around the plate. Sprinkle with the remaining fennel fronds.

Substitutions

Chicken, pork, salmon

Wine Notes

This dish requires a white wine with forward fruit and oak presence. Talbott's *Sleepy Hollow Vineyard* Chardonnay from Monterey also has a nice citrusy acidity that highlights the fennel and is not compromised by the spinach. Byron Estate and Sanford in Santa Barbara produce complementary styles as well.

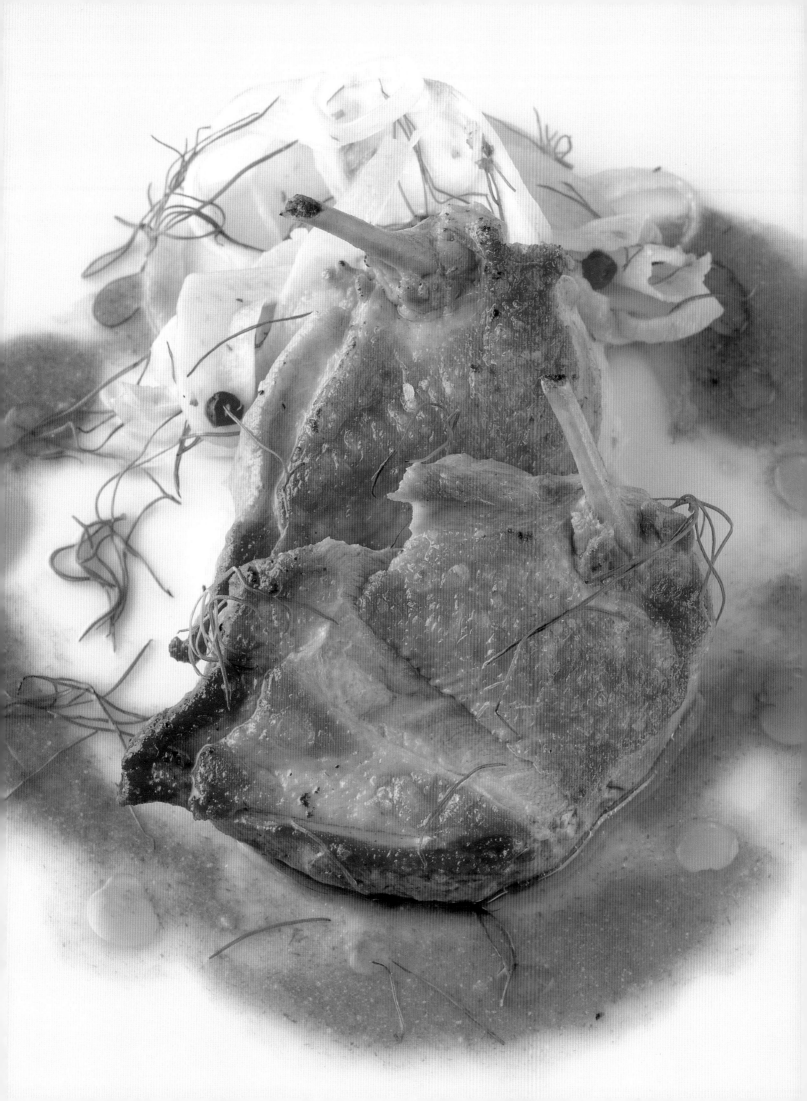

There is scarcely any living thing
    that flies in the air, swims in the sea,
or moves on the land, that is not made to
    minister to [man's] appetite in some
region or other.—PETER LUND SIMMONDS

Roasted Chestnut Soup with Foie Gras, Cipolline Onions, and Ginger

*Rich foie gras and naturally sweet chestnuts make for one of the truly great
flavor combinations. Here, chestnuts appear in three forms, allowing for a definitive study
of their flavor and texture. First, they are roasted and puréed with stock to make the soup.
Then, whole roasted pieces are used as a textural foil for the foie gras. Finally, chestnuts
are shaved over the soup to highlight their uniquely sweet, starchy flavor. Preserved Ginger
and cipolline onions add a controlled sweetness that rounds out the preparation magnificently.*

Serves 4

2 cups roasted chestnuts, shells removed

*1/2 cup Beef Stock Reduction
(see Appendices)*

2 bay leaves

3 star anise

6 allspice berries

1 shallot, minced

2 tablespoons butter

1/4 cup Madeira

3 cups Chicken Stock (see Appendices)

5 sprigs thyme

Salt and pepper

4 cipolline onions

4 2-ounce portions foie gras, cleaned

1/4 cup crème fraîche

2 tablespoons water

*4 teaspoons Preserved Ginger
(see Appendices)*

1 teaspoon fresh thyme leaves

METHOD To prepare the chestnuts: Thinly shave 4 of the chestnuts with a vegetable peeler and set aside. Quarter 1 cup of the chestnuts and place in a small saucepan with the Beef Stock Reduction, then warm just prior to serving. Chop the remaining chestnuts and set aside for the soup.

To prepare the soup: Tie the bay leaves, star anise, and allspice berries in a piece of cheesecloth, creating a sachet. Sweat the shallot in 1 tablespoon of the butter in a medium saucepan over low heat for 2 minutes, or until translucent. Add the Madeira and deglaze the pan. Add the chopped chestnuts, sachet, and Chicken Stock and cook over medium heat for 30 to 40 minutes, or until the chestnuts are very soft. Add the thyme sprigs and simmer for 2 minutes. Remove the thyme sprigs and sachet and discard. Purée the soup until smooth. Season to taste with salt and pepper.

To prepare the onions: Place the cipolline onions and the remaining 1 tablespoon butter in a small sauté pan and cook over low heat for 6 to 8 minutes, or until the onions are tender and golden brown. Quarter the onions through the stem end and season to taste with salt and pepper.

To prepare the foie gras: Season the foie gras with salt and pepper. Place in a hot sauté pan and cook over medium heat for 1 to 2 minutes on each side, or until medium-rare. Cut each portion into 3 pieces. Reserve the foie gras fat from the pan.

ASSEMBLY Combine the crème fraîche and water in a small bowl, mixing well. Ladle some of the soup into each bowl, and arrange the warm quartered chestnuts and onions around the soup. Place 3 pieces of the foie gras in the center of the soup and arrange the Preserved Ginger over the foie gras. Spoon the crème fraîche in a ring around the soup and drizzle the foie gras fat over the top. Sprinkle the shaved chestnuts and thyme leaves around the bowl.

Substitutions

Duck liver, chicken, quail, scallops

Wine Notes

A supple-textured, full-bodied New World Chardonnay accentuates the lush, velvety character of the chestnut soup. From Sonoma, the Gallo *Estate* Chardonnay, with its toasty brown spice notes and ripeness, is an elegant match.

Oxtail-and-Foie Gras–Stuffed Poached Breast of Chicken with Chicken Consommé and Savoy Cabbage

Although this dish is fairly light, a sensual lustiness pervades it as well.
The chicken breast meat melts like butter, but it is given a sturdiness with its filling, oxtail meat
and foie gras. The texture and flavor of the savoy cabbage and tiny leeks provide the
ideal foil—a humble earthiness—to the meat. Mushrooms add just the right toothsome texture,
and the clean, balanced consommé is the perfect bath for these lovely, complementary components
to swim in. For a variation, try substituting a shellfish consommé.

Serves 4

2 organic chicken breasts, boned and skinned

Salt and pepper

1½ cups loosely packed spinach, blanched and shocked

½ cup Braised Oxtail (see Appendices)

2 ounces foie gras, cleaned

Pinch of saffron threads

3 tablespoons butter

1½ cups chopped savoy cabbage

1 tablespoon rice vinegar

4 tiny leeks, cut into 2-inch pieces on the diagonal

½ cup water

1 cup small chanterelle mushrooms, cleaned

1 teaspoon chopped shallot

4 cups Chicken Consommé (see Appendices)

2 star anise

2 tablespoons julienned dried apricots

4 teaspoons olive oil

4 teaspoons Basil Oil (see Appendices)

12 micro fennel sprouts

8 young sprigs thyme

METHOD To prepare the chicken: Lay the chicken breasts on a cutting board lined with plastic wrap. Place another piece of plastic wrap over the chicken and gently pound with a mallet to flatten. Season the chicken breasts with salt and pepper. Lay half of the spinach in the center of each chicken breast and top with ¼ cup of the Braised Oxtail meat.

Season the foie gras with salt and pepper. Place in a hot sauté pan and sear over medium-high heat for 45 seconds on each side, or until golden brown. Cool to room temperature and chop coarsely.

Place half of the foie gras over the oxtail meat. Roll up the chicken breast into a cigar shape using the plastic wrap to pull it tight. Tightly wrap the stuffed chicken breast with plastic wrap and then in aluminum foil. Refrigerate the stuffed chicken breasts for 1 hour.

Place the aluminum foil-wrapped chicken breasts in a pot of barely simmering water (195 to 200 degrees) and poach for 15 minutes, turning halfway through cooking. Allow the chicken to rest for 2 minutes, remove the aluminum foil and plastic wrap, and cut each breast into 8 slices.

To prepare the cabbage: Place the saffron in a small sauté pan and cook over medium heat for 20 seconds. Add 1 tablespoon of the butter and the cabbage and cook for 3 minutes. Add the rice vinegar, cover, and cook over medium-low heat for 7 to 10 minutes, or until the cabbage is tender. Season to taste with salt and pepper.

To prepare the leeks: Place the leeks in a small sauté pan with 1 tablespoon of the butter and cook over medium heat for 3 minutes. Add the water and cook for 7 to 10 minutes, or until the leeks are tender. Season to taste with salt and pepper.

To prepare the mushrooms: Sauté the mushrooms and shallot with the remaining 1 tablespoon butter in a sauté pan over medium heat for 3 to 5 minutes, or until tender. Season to taste with salt and pepper.

To prepare the consommé: Bring the consommé to a simmer in a medium saucepan over medium-low heat. Add the star anise, cover, and remove from the heat. Let steep for 2 minutes and remove the star anise.

ASSEMBLY Place some of the cabbage, leeks, mushrooms, and apricots in the center of each shallow bowl. Arrange 4 slices of the stuffed chicken over the vegetables and ladle in the hot consommé. Drizzle the olive oil and Basil Oil around the bowl. Sprinkle with the fennel sprouts and thyme and top with freshly ground black pepper.

Substitutions

Poussin, pork, veal

Wine Notes

The oxtail and foie gras take the poached chicken to a higher level. The saffron in the cabbage continues the ascent. New World Semillon, like l'École No. 41 from Washington State, is an aromatic match for the saffron and full bodied enough to handle the stuffed chicken breasts. Cool, fruity Gamay from the Touraine is another possibility here. The soft tannins and dark fruit draw out the richness of the oxtail meat and the fruity character of the chanterelle mushrooms.

Grilled Pheasant Breast with Wild Strawberries, Pistachios, and Apricot-Curry Sauce

This playful dish contrasts the sweet, slightly tangy berry flavor with the crunchy rich pistachio pieces, using the mild but sturdy flavor of the pheasant breast as a backdrop. Delicately flavored leeks nestled beneath the meat provide the ideal, slightly resistant texture, and a mildly pungent Apricot-Curry Sauce adds an exotic overtone. Although the preparation is light and clean, the flavors and textures are decisive and satisfying.

Serves 4

4 tiny leeks

2 teaspoons butter

¾ cup Chicken Stock (see Appendices)

Salt and pepper

4 wild strawberries, stems removed and mashed

4 apricots, peeled, pitted, and cut into small dice

2 tablespoons Red Wine Reduction (see Appendices)

12 wild strawberries, stems on and halved lengthwise

2 tablespoons pistachio oil

3 pheasant breasts, boned

1 tablespoon olive oil

Apricot-Curry Sauce (recipe follows)

4 teaspoons toasted, chopped pistachios

2 teaspoons fresh spearmint chiffonade

METHOD To prepare the leeks: Place the leeks in a small saucepan with the butter and ½ cup of the Chicken Stock. Simmer the leeks over medium-low heat for 5 to 7 minutes, or until tender. Remove the leeks from the liquid and slice into 1-inch pieces on the diagonal. Season to taste with salt and pepper. Place the mashed wild strawberries in the liquid remaining in the pan that held the leeks and cook for 3 minutes. Pass through a fine-mesh sieve.

To prepare the apricots: Warm the apricots in the Red Wine Reduction and the remaining ¼ cup Chicken Stock for 5 minutes, or until the apricots are tender.

To prepare the wild strawberries: Preheat the oven to 325 degrees. Toss the cut wild strawberries with 2 teaspoons of the pistachio oil and place in an ovenproof pan. Heat the strawberries in the oven for 10 minutes, or until warm.

To prepare the pheasant: Season the pheasant with salt and pepper and rub with the olive oil. Grill the pheasant over a medium flame for 4 minutes on each side, or until just cooked. Remove from the grill and let rest for 3 minutes. Thinly slice the pheasant to yield 20 slices. Season to taste with salt and pepper.

ASSEMBLY Arrange some of the leeks and diced apricots in the center of each plate. Lay 5 pheasant slices over the leeks and apricots. Spoon some of the Apricot-Curry Sauce, mashed wild strawberry mixture, and any juices from the apricots around the plate. Arrange the warm strawberries around the pheasant. Sprinkle with the pistachios and spearmint. Drizzle the remaining 4 teaspoons pistachio oil around the plate and top with freshly ground black pepper.

Apricot-Curry Sauce

Yield: 2½ cups

¾ cup dried apricots

1½ teaspoons hot curry powder

½ cup rice vinegar

1⅓ cups water

METHOD Purée all the ingredients in a food processor for 3 minutes, or until smooth. Refrigerate overnight and pass through a fine-mesh sieve. Refrigerate the sauce until ready to use or for up to 1 week.

Substitutions

Pork, chicken, poussin

Wine Notes

This preparation is given a spicy hit by the curry, which contrasts with the raspy wild strawberries and tart apricot. Young Beaujolais from a more aromatic and elegant cru, such as seductive Fleurie or fragrant Chiroubles with pure fruit expression, harmonizes the spice and tart elements without adding too much density to this dish.

Poussin with Duck Gizzard, Baby Fennel, and Black Truffle Stew, and Pinot Noir Emulsion

*Poussin is light and delicate in flavor and works best with elements
that don't overpower it. Here, an aromatic stew of duck gizzards, baby fennel, and black
truffles certainly asserts itself, but not so much so that the bird succumbs. A barely
astringent Pinot Noir Emulsion further melds these ideally matched components together.
A little meat juice provides a nice richness to finish the plate.*

Serves 4

1/2 cup chopped bacon

4 cups loosely packed chopped collard greens

1 tablespoon brown sugar

2 tablespoons red wine vinegar

2 cups water

Salt and pepper

4 baby fennel bulbs

4 teaspoons olive oil

4 poussin breasts, boned

4 teaspoons grapeseed oil

1 black truffle, cut into small chunks

*3/4 cup Game Bird Stock Reduction
(see Appendices)*

Duck Gizzard Confit (recipe follows)

Pinot Noir Emulsion (recipe follows)

4 teaspoons fresh tiny sage leaves

METHOD To prepare the collard greens: Cook the bacon in a medium sauté pan for 5 minutes, or until the fat is rendered. Add the collard greens and cook for 3 minutes. Add the sugar, red wine vinegar, and water, cover, and cook over low heat for 1 hour, or until the greens are tender (additional water may be necessary). Season to taste with salt and pepper.

To prepare the fennel: Cook the fennel in a sauté pan with the olive oil over medium heat for 7 minutes, or until tender. Season to taste with salt and pepper and cut each fennel bulb in half.

To prepare the poussin breasts: Season the breasts with salt and pepper. Place in a hot sauté pan with the grapeseed oil and cook over medium-high heat for 5 to 7 minutes on each side, or until just cooked.

To prepare the truffles: Warm the truffle pieces with the Game Bird Stock Reduction in a small saucepan over medium heat for 3 to 5 minutes, or until hot.

ASSEMBLY Place some of the gizzards and fennel in the center of each plate. Spoon the truffle pieces and reduction sauce over the fennel. Place a poussin breast over the truffles and spoon the Pinot Noir Emulsion around the plate. Sprinkle with the sage leaves and top with freshly ground black pepper.

Duck Gizzard Confit

Yield: 8 gizzards

8 duck gizzards

1 cup coarse salt

Grapeseed oil for covering giblets

2 cloves garlic

1/2 cup chopped Spanish onion

4 sprigs thyme

1 sprig rosemary

1 bay leaf

METHOD Cover the gizzards with the coarse salt and refrigerate overnight.

Preheat the oven to 300 degrees. Rinse the salt from the giblets, place in an ovenproof pan, and cover with the grapeseed oil. Add the garlic, onion, thyme, rosemary, and bay leaf. Bake in the oven for 3 hours or, until the gizzards are tender. Cool the gizzards in the oil and cut into 1/4-inch-thick slices.

Pinot Noir Emulsion

Yield: 1/2 cup

1 Spanish onion, coarsely chopped

1 carrot, coarsely chopped

1 stalk celery, coarsely chopped

1 Granny Smith apple, coarsely chopped

2 cloves garlic

2 tablespoons grapeseed oil

1 750-ml bottle Pinot Noir

1 cup Chicken Stock (see Appendices)

3 tablespoons butter

Salt and pepper

METHOD Cook the onion, carrot, celery, apple, and garlic with the grapeseed oil in a medium sauté pan over medium heat for 10 minutes, or until golden brown and caramelized. Add the Pinot Noir and simmer over medium heat for 2 hours.

Strain and place in a small saucepan with the Chicken Stock. Continue to simmer over medium heat for 1 hour, or until reduced to 1 cup. Whisk in the butter and season to taste with salt and pepper. Froth with a handheld blender just prior to use.

Substitutions

Chicken, beef, pork, scallops

Wine Notes

The wine selection should harmonize the bubbly emulsion with the aromatic fennel, smoky bacon, and rich gizzard. A fruity Pinot Noir with soft tannin like Robert Sinskey from Carneros brings the elements together. The aromatic Cabernet Franc of the Loire Valley, particularly in the hands of a master like Charles Joguet in Chinon, with his *Les Varennes du Grand Clos*, is another excellent match for this dish.

Partridge Breast with Two Risottos, Red Wine–Black Olive Sauce, and Celery Sprouts

In this preparation, the partridge breast is backed up by two distinct but complementary risottos. One features black olives and the other radicchio and apple. A red wine–black olive sauce and a drizzle of meat juice round out the plate with depth and richness. The entire dish comes across as something lusty and full flavored and at the same time light and delicate.

Serves 4

4 shallots, chopped

6 cloves garlic, minced

4 tablespoons olive oil

1 750-ml bottle Merlot

1 cup finely chopped kalamata olives

¼ cup Vegetable Stock (see Appendices)

Salt and pepper

1 red apple, peeled and cut into small wedges

5 tablespoons butter

2 tablespoons sherry wine vinegar

1 cup water

¾ cup arborio rice

2¼ cups Chicken Stock (see Appendices)

¼ cup kalamata olives, coarsely chopped

¼ cup grated Parmesan cheese

2 tablespoons fresh flat-leaf parsley chiffonade

1 small head radicchio, quartered lengthwise

¼ cup peeled, julienned apple

2 partridge, trussed

8 sprigs thyme

½ cup Meat Stock Reduction, hot (see Appendices)

8 teaspoons micro celery sprouts

METHOD To prepare the olive sauce: Sweat the shallots and garlic in 2 tablespoons of the olive oil in a large saucepan over medium heat for 2 minutes. Add the Merlot and simmer over medium heat for 30 minutes, or until reduced to ¼ cup. Add the finely chopped olives and the Vegetable Stock and purée until smooth. Season to taste with pepper.

To prepare the apple: Cook the red apple wedges with 1 tablespoon of the butter in a medium sauté pan over medium heat for 3 minutes, or until they begin to brown. Add the sherry wine vinegar and cook until dry. Add the water and cook for 5 minutes, or until the apple is tender. Mash the apple slightly with a fork just prior to serving.

To prepare the risotto: Melt 2 tablespoons of the butter in a large sauté pan over medium heat, add the rice, and cook for 2 minutes, stirring frequently. Slowly add ¼ cup of the Chicken Stock and stir until completely absorbed. Add the remaining 2 cups stock, ¼ cup at a time, stirring continuously with a smooth, gentle motion until the liquid is completely absorbed before adding more. (The risotto will take 40 to 50 minutes to cook completely.)

To prepare the black olive risotto: Fold the coarsely chopped olives, 2 tablespoons of the Parmesan cheese, and the parsley into half of the warm risotto and season to taste with salt and pepper.

To prepare the radicchio risotto: Place the radicchio in a sauté pan with the remaining 2 tablespoons butter and cook over medium heat for 10 minutes, or until tender. Coarsely chop the radicchio and season to taste with salt and pepper. Fold the radicchio, julienned apple, and the remaining 2 tablespoons Parmesan cheese into the remaining risotto and season to taste with salt and pepper.

To prepare the partridge: Preheat the oven to 350 degrees. Season the inside cavity and outside of each partridge with salt and pepper. Place 4 sprigs of thyme in the cavity of each partridge. Brush the partridge with the remaining 2 tablespoons olive oil and sear them in a hot sauté pan over medium-high heat for 2 to 3 minutes on each side, or until golden brown. Transfer the partridge to a roasting pan and roast for 10 to 12 minutes, or until the partridge are just cooked. Remove from the oven and let rest for 5 minutes. Remove the breasts from the bodies and thinly slice. Reserve the remaining parts of the partridge for another use.

ASSEMBLY Place some of the mashed apple in the center of each plate and arrange the partridge meat over the apple. Spoon the olive risotto on the right side of the plate and the radicchio risotto on the left side of the plate. Spoon the olive sauce around the plate. Spoon the Meat Stock Reduction over the partridge and top with freshly ground black pepper. Sprinkle the micro celery sprouts around the plate.

Substitutions

Chicken, beef, squab

Wine Notes

The kalamata olives and radicchio provide the piquant kick for both the risotto and the partridge. A polished red without too much oaky vanillin, like Chappellet's Sangiovese from Napa Valley, does not bow before the intensity of the olives. Neither does it interfere with the creamy texture of the risotto.

Robust Poultry
& Other Fowl

Grouse Breast with Organic Root Vegetables and Legume Sauces

*Grouse is heady and full flavored, which is why it works wonderfully with elements
that are sturdy but won't compete with it. Here, several root vegetables offer up their sweet yet
masculine flavors to offset the rich bird, and the earthy, almost-creamy legume sauces help to tame
the dish. Herb notes, aged balsamic vinegar, and grouse reduction round out things nicely.*

Serves 4

¾ cup large-chopped bacon

1 cup large-chopped celery

1 cup large-chopped carrot

1½ cups large-chopped Spanish onion

*½ cup dried black beans, soaked in water
overnight*

*1 jalapeño chile, halved lengthwise
and seeded*

*½ cup dried garbanzo beans, soaked in
water overnight*

1 teaspoon curry powder

⅓ cup fresh adzuki beans

1 sprig rosemary

4½ cups water

5½ tablespoons butter

Salt and pepper

*½ cup shelled fava beans,
parboiled and peeled*

½ cup Vegetable Stock (see Appendices)

20 crosnes, cleaned

4 baby red carrots

8 baby golden beets

8 baby turnips, peeled

2 grouse, trussed

1 tablespoon grapeseed oil

1 teaspoon chopped fresh sage

2 teaspoons finely cut fresh chives

4 teaspoons 25-year-old balsamic vinegar

4 teaspoons Herb Oil (see Appendices)

*½ cup Grouse Stock Reduction, hot
(see Appendices)*

4 teaspoons fresh chervil leaves

METHOD To prepare the sauces: Place
¼ cup of the bacon in each of 3 small
saucepans and cook over medium heat for
5 minutes, or until the fat is rendered.
Evenly divide the celery, carrot, and onion
among the pans and cook over medium-
high heat for 3 minutes, or until golden
brown. Place the black beans and jalapeño
in the first saucepan, place the garbanzo
beans and curry powder in the second
saucepan, and place the adzuki beans
and rosemary in the third saucepan. Add
1½ cups of the water and 1½ tablespoons of
the butter to each pan and simmer over
medium-low heat for 1 to 1½ hours, or until
the beans are tender. Remove the bacon,
vegetables, and rosemary from the pans
and discard. Purée the beans separately
with enough of their cooking liquid to
make thin purées. Season to taste with salt
and pepper.

Purée the fava beans with enough of the
Vegetable Stock to create a thin purée.
Season to taste with salt and pepper. Warm
the fava bean purée just prior to serving.

To prepare the vegetables: Cook the crosnes
in boiling salted water for 3 to 4 minutes, or
until al dente. Season to taste with salt and
pepper. Cook the carrots in boiling salted
water for 3 to 4 minutes, or until al dente.
Season to taste with salt and pepper.
Simmer the beets in salted water for
10 minutes, or until the skin easily comes
off. Remove from the water and remove the
skins and stems. Season to taste with salt
and pepper. Place the turnips in a hot sauté
pan with the remaining 1 tablespoon butter
and cook over medium heat for 6 to 8 minutes, or until tender. Season to taste with
salt and pepper.

To prepare the grouse: Preheat the oven to
400 degrees. Season the grouse with salt
and pepper. Place the grouse in a hot sauté
pan with the grapeseed oil and sear on all
sides for 1 to 2 minutes, or until golden
brown. Roast the grouse in the oven for
20 to 30 minutes, or until cooked. Remove
the breasts from the bone, and slice each
breast into 5 pieces. Season to taste with
salt and pepper. (Reserve the remaining
parts of the grouse for another use.)

ASSEMBLY Spoon some of the fava bean
purée across the top of each plate, and continue down the plate with the black bean,
garbanzo bean, and adzuki bean purées.
Place 2 pieces of carrot on the left end of
the fava bean purée and sprinkle with
the sage. Place 2 beets on the left end of
the black bean purée and sprinkle with the
chives. Place 2 turnips on the left end of
the garbanzo bean purée and drizzle with
the balsamic vinegar. Place 5 crosnes on the
left end of the adzuki bean purée and drizzle with the Herb Oil. Arrange 5 slices of
the grouse at the opposite side of the plate
and drizzle the Grouse Stock Reduction
over and around the grouse. Sprinkle with
the chervil and top with freshly ground
black pepper.

Substitutions

Squab, chicken, duck

Wine Notes

In this dish, the turnips, carrots, and beets
all have a natural sweetness that pairs
nicely with the rich, creamy beans. A white
wine with good intensity and a long finish
is required here, and Savennières, a Chenin
Blanc from the Loire Valley, fits. The *Clos
du Papillon* from Domaine des Baumard
and *Clos de la Coulée-de-Serrant* from
Nicholas Joly are the best examples of this
type of Savennières.

Peppered Squab Breast with Its Liver in Tempura, Steel-Cut Oats, Braised Rhubarb, and Vanilla Gastricque

*This dish features several complex flavors and textures, but they all come together quite nicely.
The plump nuggets of squab breast have just the right heat from the pepper.
The liver of the bird adds an intensity and, because it is battered and lightly fried, a delicate crispness.
Rhubarb, with its elegant tartness, is a wonderful contrast to the barely sweet vanilla in the
gastricque, both of which further accentuate the squab. Finally, steel-cut oats add a creaminess that
gives this preparation just the richness that it needs. Micro greens are the only final accent needed.*

Serves 4

1 cup steel-cut rolled oats, soaked in water overnight

2 tablespoons minced shallot

¼ habanero chile, seeded and minced

1 tablespoon plus 1 teaspoon butter

2¾ cups plus 1 tablespoon water

½ cup milk

2 tablespoons coarsely chopped fresh flat-leaf parsley

Salt and pepper

¾ cup flour

1¼ teaspoons baking powder

1 egg

3 egg whites, whipped to medium-stiff peaks

Grapeseed oil for deep-frying

4 squab livers, cleaned

⅓ cup sugar

Pulp of ¼ vanilla bean

2 teaspoons rice vinegar

2 stalks rhubarb

⅓ cup Chicken Stock (see Appendices)

2 squabs, trussed

4 sprigs thyme

1 tablespoon grapeseed oil

½ cup Squab Stock Reduction, hot (see Appendices)

2 tablespoons micro cilantro sprouts

METHOD To prepare the oatmeal: Drain the water from the rolled oats. Sweat the shallot and habanero chile in 1 teaspoon of the butter in a small saucepan for 1 minute. Add the rolled oats and 2½ cups of the water and simmer over medium-low heat for 30 minutes, or until tender. Add the milk and parsley and cook for 5 minutes. Season to taste with salt and pepper.

To prepare the tempura: Place the flour and baking powder in a large bowl. Whisk in the egg and ¼ cup of the water and season to taste with salt and pepper. Fold the flour mixture into the egg mixture, then fold in the egg whites. (The tempura batter must be used within 30 minutes after the addition of the egg whites.)

Pour the grapeseed oil to a depth of 2 inches in a saucepan and preheat the oil to 375 degrees. Season the livers with salt and pepper. Dip the livers into the tempura batter, completely coating each liver, and slip into the hot oil. Cook for 2 minutes on each side, or until lightly golden brown. Drain on paper towels and season with salt and pepper. Cut each piece of tempura into 3 slices.

To prepare the gastricque: Place the sugar, the remaining 1 tablespoon water, and the vanilla bean pulp in a small saucepan. Cook over medium heat without stirring for 5 minutes, or until the sugar is caramelized. Add the rice vinegar and cook for 2 minutes.

To prepare the rhubarb: Cut the red outer portion from the rhubarb and cut into a small dice. Sauté the rhubarb in the remaining 1 tablespoon butter in a sauté pan for 3 minutes. Add the Chicken Stock and cook over medium-low heat for 5 minutes, or until tender. Season to taste with salt and pepper.

To prepare the squabs: Preheat the oven to 375 degrees. Season the squabs with salt and pepper. Place 2 thyme sprigs in the cavity of each bird. Sear the squabs with the grapeseed oil in a hot sauté pan over medium-high heat for 3 minutes on each side, or until golden brown. Roast the squabs for 10 minutes, or until cooked medium-rare. Let rest for 5 minutes. Remove the breasts from the bones and cut each breast into 4 pieces. Season to taste with salt and pepper. (Reserve the remaining parts of the squab for another use.)

ASSEMBLY Fold half of the cooked rhubarb into the oatmeal and spoon down the center of each plate. Arrange the sliced squab and squab liver tempura slices over the oatmeal. Spoon the remaining rhubarb over the oatmeal and around the plate. Spoon the gastricque and the Squab Stock Reduction around the plate and sprinkle with the micro cilantro sprouts. Top with freshly ground black pepper.

Substitutions

Chicken, duck, scallops

Wine Notes

The juxtaposition of sweet and tart elements paired with the very dense oatmeal and the rich squab is handled well by the aromatic Rhône varietal Viognier. As high acidity in wine overmagnifies the tartness of the rhubarb, and sweetness in the wine overmagnifies the vanilla and caramel, a richly textured, dry style with naturally lower acidity is the way to maintain the balance. John Alban provides the right wine, Alban *Estate* Viognier from Edna Valley in California.

Black Chicken with Its Liver, White Corn Grits, Crispy Pancetta, and Hen of the Woods Mushrooms

Black chicken, with full flavor and meaty texture, stands up beautifully to the rich and hearty elements. Here, it is partnered with its liver to accentuate its lusty flavor. Hen of the woods mushrooms provide a clean earthiness, while their purée adds a gorgeous mouthfeel. The creamy richness of white corn grits is a perfect textural foil for the pancetta. In the end, the preparation is at once remarkably rustic and highly refined.

Serves 4

4 thin slices pancetta

½ cup julienned pancetta

½ cup diced Spanish onion

6 tablespoons butter

1 cup white corn grits

2½ cups water

2 tablespoons sherry wine vinegar

Salt and pepper

2 black chickens, trussed

4 sprigs thyme

4 cloves garlic

4 tablespoons olive oil

1 shallot, minced

2 cups hen of the woods mushrooms, cleaned

4 baby fennel bulbs, halved lengthwise

4 chicken livers, cleaned

¼ cup loosely packed micro arugula sprouts

½ cup Meat Stock Reduction, hot (see Appendices)

4 teaspoons Herb Oil (see Appendices)

METHOD To prepare the crispy pancetta: Preheat the oven to 400 degrees. Lay the slices of pancetta on a parchment-lined sheet pan. Cover with a second sheet of parchment and top with another sheet pan. Bake, checking frequently, for 20 minutes, or until golden brown and crispy. Cool on the parchment paper and carefully remove just prior to serving.

To prepare the grits: Place the julienned pancetta in a saucepan and cook over medium heat for 3 minutes, or until the fat is rendered. Add the onion and cook for 5 minutes, or until translucent. Add 3 tablespoons of the butter and the grits and cook for 1 minute, or until the grits are coated with the fat. Add 2 cups of the water and cook over very low heat, stirring occasionally, for 1 hour, or until very tender. Add the sherry wine vinegar and season to taste with salt and pepper.

To prepare the chickens: Preheat the oven to 375 degrees. Season the chickens with salt and pepper and place 2 sprigs of the thyme and 2 garlic cloves in the cavity of each chicken. Brush the chickens with olive oil and roast for 40 minutes, or until the juices run clear. Let rest for 5 minutes. Remove the breasts from the bone and cut each breast into 3 pieces. Season to taste with salt and pepper. (Reserve the remaining parts of the chicken for another use.)

To prepare the mushrooms: Sweat the shallot with 1 tablespoon of the butter in a small sauté pan over medium heat for 1 minute. Add the mushrooms and cook over medium heat for 5 minutes, or until tender. Season to taste with salt and pepper. Purée one-third of the mushrooms with the remaining ½ cup water until smooth. Heat the purée in a small saucepan over medium heat for 2 minutes and season to taste with salt and pepper.

To prepare the fennel: Place the fennel bulbs in a hot sauté pan with 1 tablespoon of the butter and cook over medium heat for 5 to 7 minutes, or until caramelized and tender. Season to taste with salt and pepper.

To prepare the chicken livers: Season the livers with salt and pepper. Place the livers in a hot sauté pan with the remaining 1 tablespoon butter and cook over medium-high heat for 1 minute on each side, or until cooked medium-rare. Slice each liver into 2 pieces on the diagonal and season to taste with salt and pepper.

ASSEMBLY Spoon some of the grits into the center of each plate and arrange the fennel and chicken livers over the grits. Arrange the mushrooms next to the livers and lay 3 slices of the black chicken over the mushrooms. Spoon the mushroom purée around the plate and spoon the Meat Stock Reduction over the chicken. Place a piece of crispy pancetta standing up in the grits and sprinkle the arugula sprouts around the chicken. Drizzle the Herb Oil around the plate and top with freshly ground black pepper.

Substitutions

Chicken, pork, squab

Wine Notes

The black chicken, hen of the woods mushrooms, and pancetta lend exoticism and luxury to normally humble grits. A full-flavored Chardonnay is in order here. Jim Clendenen's Burgundian-influenced Au Bon Climat *Talley Vineyard Reserve* embraces the ripe fruit of California and packages it in French oak. The creamy grits, crispy pancetta, and crisp-skinned chicken work well with this rounded Chardonnay.

Honey-Coriander-and Fennel-Glazed Capon
with Gnocchi, Black Truffles, and Crosnes

The flavor of capon is fairly mild, but the texture is somewhat dense. Thus, it is perfectly suited
to the delicate aromatic enhancement of coriander and ginger. Here, the meat is additionally paired with
meltaway gnocchi, pungent slices of black truffle, and toothsome porcini mushroom pieces.
Just-crunchy crosnes provide a slightly resistant texture that acts as a desirable foil to the meat.
Mushroom juice helps to keep these heady, regal flavors splendidly light and clean.

Serves 4

½ cup bacon lardons

⅔ cup crosnes, cleaned and parboiled

2½ cups Mushroom Stock (see Appendices)

2 cups Roasted Porcini Mushrooms,
cut into sixths (see Appendices)

1 small black truffle, thinly sliced

2 teaspoons chopped fresh sage

1 tablespoon butter

Salt and pepper

¼ cup honey

4 teaspoons coriander seeds, coarsely ground

2 tablespoons fennel seeds

4 teaspoons minced fresh ginger

2 capon breasts, boned

Gnocchi (recipe follows)

4 teaspoons truffle oil

METHOD To prepare the ragout: Cook the bacon in a large sauté pan over medium heat for 5 minutes, or until the fat is rendered. Add the crosnes and cook for 3 minutes. Add 2 cups of the Mushroom Stock and simmer for 5 minutes, or until the stock is reduced by half. Add the mushrooms, truffle slices, sage, and butter and season to taste with salt and pepper.

To prepare the capon breasts: Combine the honey, coriander, fennel seeds, ginger, and the remaining ½ cup Mushroom Stock. Season the capon breasts with salt and pepper. Place the breasts, skin side down, in a hot nonstick sauté pan over medium heat for 4 minutes, or until golden brown. Turn over, and brush with some of the glaze. Cook for 7 minutes, or until just done. Brush the cooked capon with the remaining glaze, and cut each breast in half crosswise. Season to taste with salt and pepper.

ASSEMBLY Spoon some of the ragout in the center of each plate. Place some of the gnocchi over the ragout and top with a piece of the capon. Drizzle the truffle oil around the plate and top with freshly ground black pepper.

Gnocchi

Yield: approximately 4 dozen

2½ pounds Idaho potatoes, boiled and riced

1 egg

1 teaspoon salt

1 to 1½ cups flour

1 teaspoon butter

Salt and pepper

METHOD Place the hot riced potato in a large bowl. Work the egg, 1 teaspoon salt, and ½ cup of the flour into the potato with a wooden spoon. Knead in enough of the remaining flour to form a silky, soft dough.

Divide the dough into 4 equal portions, and roll each portion into a long cigar shape about ½ inch in diameter. Cut the rolls into ½-inch pieces and gently pinch each piece in the center. Refrigerate on a lightly floured sheet pan until ready to cook.

Poach the gnocchi in boiling salted water for 2 to 3 minutes, or just until they float. Transfer the gnocchi to a large bowl with a slotted spoon. Toss with the butter and season to taste with salt and pepper.

Substitutions

Pheasant, chicken, beef

Wine Notes

The delicate flesh of the capon is fortified with a dose of anise and with sweetness from the coriander and honey. This dish straddles the fence between white and red Burgundy, and the earthy edge delivered by the mushrooms and black truffles does nothing to tip the scales. A powerful style of Chassagne-Montrachet such as *Ruchottes* from Ramonet weaves itself into the course and becomes a seamless pairing. A more exciting match, however, is a mature red Burgundy like the suave grand crus of Morey St. Denis. The silky, dark fruit *Clos de la Roche* from Domaine Dujac adds another dimension of richness to the dish.

Squab Breast with Fiddlehead Ferns, Ramps, and Star Anise Vinaigrette

~~~~~~

This preparation evokes spring, with lean, yet succulent squab meat resting next to a medley
of crispy, nutty, almost-sweet fiddlehead ferns; toothsome, caramelized tiny round carrots;
and herbaceous, pleasantly grasslike ramps. But it is not only the vegetables' flavors that so marvelously
complement and contrast with the meat; their respective textures brilliantly do the same.
A star anise vinaigrette adds an exotic flavor note to make the overall effect of this dish pleasantly provocative.

Serves 4

1 1/2 teaspoons ground star anise

3 tablespoons freshly squeezed lemon juice

1/4 cup plus 2 tablespoons grapeseed oil

1/4 cup olive oil

Salt and pepper

8 round carrots, stems trimmed

1 tablespoon butter

2 squabs, trussed

20 fiddlehead ferns, parboiled

8 ramps, blanched

2 tablespoons fennel sprouts

METHOD To prepare the vinaigrette: Whisk together the star anise and lemon juice in a small bowl. Slowly whisk in 1/4 cup of the grapeseed oil and the olive oil and season to taste with salt and pepper.

To prepare the carrots: Preheat the oven to 350 degrees. Place the carrots in a roasting pan with the butter and roast for 20 to 30 minutes, or until tender. Slice the larger carrots in half lengthwise and season to taste with salt and pepper.

To prepare the squabs: Preheat the oven to 400 degrees. Season the squabs with salt and pepper. Place the squabs in a hot sauté pan with 2 tablespoons grapeseed oil and sear over medium heat for 1 minute on each side, or until golden brown. Roast for 8 minutes, or until medium-rare. Let rest for 5 minutes. Remove the breasts from the bone and cut each breast into 1/2-inch-thick slices. Season to taste with salt and pepper. (Reserve the remaining parts of the squabs for another use.)

To prepare the fiddlehead ferns and ramps: Place the fiddlehead ferns, ramps, and 3 tablespoons of the vinaigrette in a medium sauté pan and cook for 5 minutes, or until warm. Season to taste with salt and pepper.

ASSEMBLY Arrange some of the fiddlehead ferns, ramps, and carrots on each plate. Shingle 5 slices of the squab in the center of each plate and spoon the vinaigrette around the plate. Sprinkle the fennel sprouts around the plate and top with freshly ground black pepper.

Substitutions

Chicken, beef

Wine Notes

While the vegetables in this dish point to a white wine, the rich squab meat pushes the whole toward a red. A spicy, fruit-focused Pinot Noir from Oregon brings all of the elements together. The *Evenstad Reserve* from Domaine Serene is a perennial favorite at the restaurant for its beguiling bouquet and velvety texture. The wine maker, Ken Wright, also produces the equally suitable *Guadalupe Vineyard* Pinot Noir under his own eponymous label.

Turkey Breast with Bigoli Pasta and Giblet–Foie Gras Sauce

~~~~~~

Sometimes it's fun to pair something clean, simple, and straightforward, like turkey breast, with something rich and opulent, like foie gras and varietal meats, to produce stunning flavor contrast. Here, toothsome bigoli makes a memorable stage for the turkey, providing an element that is more about texture than flavor. Lightly wilted spinach adds a necessary foil for the other richer, fuller components. Pig's feet or tails would also be a welcome addition.

Serves 4

1 small turkey with giblets (about 8 pounds)

1 cup coarse salt

Grapeseed oil for the giblets

2 cloves garlic

½ cup chopped Spanish onion

10 sprigs thyme

1 sprig rosemary

1 bay leaf

1 bulb garlic

Salt and pepper

2 tablespoons olive oil

5 ounces foie gras, cleaned

1 cup Meat Stock Reduction (see Appendices)

2½ cups flour

2 eggs

1 egg yolk

2 tablespoons milk

3½ tablespoons butter

1½ tablespoons whole-grain mustard

2 cups loosely packed baby spinach

METHOD To prepare the giblets: Cover the giblets with the coarse salt and refrigerate overnight. Preheat the oven to 300 degrees. Rinse the salt from the giblets, place in an ovenproof pan, and cover with grapeseed oil. Add the garlic, onion, 4 sprigs of the thyme, the rosemary, and the bay leaf. Cook in the oven for 3 hours, or until tender. Cool the giblets in the oil and chop coarsely.

To prepare the turkey: Preheat the oven to 325 degrees. Place the garlic bulb and the remaining 6 sprigs thyme in the cavity of the turkey. Season the cavity and the outside of the turkey with salt and pepper. Brush the turkey with the olive oil and roast, basting occasionally, for 3 hours, or until it reaches an internal temperature of 170 degrees. Let rest for 5 minutes. Remove the breast from the bone, and cut into twelve ¼-inch-thick slices. Season to taste with salt and pepper. (Reserve the remaining parts for another use.)

To prepare the foie gras: Season the foie gras with salt and pepper. Place in a hot sauté pan and cook for 1 minute on each side, or until just cooked. Cool to room temperature and cut into small dice.

To prepare the sauce: Place the Meat Stock Reduction in a small saucepan and add the foie gras and giblets. Warm over medium heat just prior to serving.

To prepare the bigoli pasta: Place the flour, eggs, egg yolk, milk, 1½ tablespoons of the butter, and the mustard in the bowl of an electric mixer. Mix with the paddle attachment on low speed until incorporated. Knead the pasta into a ball, wrap airtight with plastic wrap, and refrigerate for 3 hours. Extrude the dough from a pasta machine using the largest spaghetti setting. Cook in boiling salted water for 3 minutes, or until al dente. Drain the pasta and place in a sauté pan with 1 tablespoon of the butter. Cook for 1 minute, add half of the giblet sauce, and season with salt and pepper.

To prepare the spinach: Place the spinach in a sauté pan with the remaining 1 tablespoon butter and cook over medium heat for 3 minutes, or until wilted. Season with salt and pepper.

ASSEMBLY Arrange some of the spinach and pasta in the center of each plate. Place 3 slices of the turkey over the pasta and spoon the giblet sauce around the plate. Top with freshly ground black pepper.

Substitutions

Chicken, pork, scallops

Wine Notes

The giblet–foie gras sauce constitutes the richest component to contend with in this dish, and a fleshy Pinot Noir handles it well. Choose a style that exhibits plump fruit without big tannin, which would overpower the succulent turkey meat, or unripe acidity, which would fight with the spinach. California's Étude Pinot Noir from Carneros is one that will shine.

Roasted Partridge with Caramelized Salsify Purée, Wilted Chard, and Hen of the Woods Mushrooms

~~~~~~

Whenever a meat is roasted on the bone, the result is considerably more tender and succulent.
This is especially true for lean birds like partridge or pheasant. Here, partridge breast
is roasted, sliced, and served with a caramelized salsify purée and hen of the woods mushrooms,
flavors that are earthy yet delicate. Adzuki beans and bacon pieces deliver more
substance but, again, not overpowering flavors. Finally, wilted Swiss chard provides a clean,
astringent element that weaves everything together. The composition here, although
very much in balance, still headlines the bird as the star.

Serves 4

½ cup large-chopped Spanish onion

¼ cup large-chopped carrot

¼ cup large-chopped celery

6 tablespoons butter

1 cup dried adzuki beans, soaked in water overnight

2½ cups water

Salt and pepper

1 stalk salsify, peeled

1 cup milk

2 partridge, trussed

8 ounces slab bacon, cut into thick batons

1 tablespoon minced shallot

1½ cups hen of the woods mushrooms, cleaned

4 leaves Swiss chard, stems removed and cut into wide julienne

½ cup Partridge Stock Reduction, hot (see Appendices)

1 sprig rosemary, leaves picked

METHOD To prepare the adzuki beans: Cook the onion, carrot, and celery with 1 tablespoon of the butter in a medium saucepan over medium heat for 5 to 7 minutes, or until golden brown. Add the adzuki beans, 2 tablespoons of the butter, and the water and simmer over medium-low heat for 1½ hours, or until the beans are tender. Using a slotted spoon, remove half of the beans and set aside. Remove and discard the vegetables from the remaining beans, then purée the beans with enough of the cooking liquid to create a smooth purée. Season to taste with salt and pepper.

To prepare the salsify: Poach the salsify in the milk in a small saucepan over medium heat for 10 to 15 minutes, or until tender. Remove the salsify and cool to room temperature. Cut the salsify into 2-inch pieces. Cook the salsify with 1½ tablespoons of the butter in a small sauté pan over medium-high heat for 3 to 4 minutes, or until golden brown. Purée the salsify with just enough water to create a smooth purée. Season to taste with salt and pepper and warm just prior to serving.

To prepare the partridge: Preheat the oven to 400 degrees. Season the partridge with salt and pepper and roast in the oven for 12 to 15 minutes, or until cooked. Remove the breasts from the bone, and cut each breast in half on the diagonal. Season to taste with salt and pepper. (Reserve the remaining parts of the partridge for another use.)

To prepare the mushrooms: Cook the bacon in a small sauté pan over medium heat for 5 to 7 minutes, or until crispy. Remove the bacon pieces from the pan and discard half of the fat. Add the shallot to the pan and cook for 30 seconds. Add the mushrooms and cook for 3 to 4 minutes, or until tender. Season to taste with salt and pepper.

To prepare the Swiss chard: Place the Swiss chard and the remaining 1½ tablespoons butter in a small sauté pan over medium heat and cook for 3 to 4 minutes, or until wilted. Season to taste with salt and pepper.

ASSEMBLY Arrange some of the Swiss chard in the center of each plate. Place 2 pieces of partridge standing up in the chard. Spoon the salsify purée around the partridge. Arrange the adzuki beans, bacon batons, and mushrooms around the plate. Spoon the adzuki purée around the plate and drizzle the Partridge Stock Reduction over the partridge and vegetables. Sprinkle with the rosemary leaves and top with freshly ground black pepper.

Substitutions

Chicken, beef, scallops

Wine Notes

Richly flavored partridge, earthy adzuki beans with smoky bacon, and the scent of rosemary point to a meaty red. Mourvèdre-based *Homage à Jacques Perrin* from Château de Beaucastel is a blockbuster Châteauneuf-du-Pape smelling of smoked meats and black fruits. It is a heady wine that takes this dish to another level.

Squab with Roasted Garlic Risotto, Red Wine Reduction, and Chanterelle Mushrooms and Their Purée

The squab is beautifully complemented by the creamy and evocative roasted garlic risotto
and the delicately earthy, strawlike chanterelle mushrooms. Only a little Red Wine Reduction
is needed to rovide a fruity, lightly acidic note to help cut into the rich ingredients that
make up the dish. Chive and black pepper also help to tame these majestically bold flavors.

Serves 4

4 squab legs

Salt and pepper

2 tablespoons grapeseed oil

1/4 cup chopped carrot

1/4 cup chopped leek

1/4 cup chopped Spanish onion

1/2 cup chopped celery

1 teaspoon tomato paste

1/2 cup red wine

2 cloves garlic

5 1/2 cups Chicken Stock (see Appendices)

1 Spanish onion, julienned

6 tablespoons butter

2 teaspoons minced garlic

1/2 cup minced Spanish onion

1 cup arborio rice

2 tablespoons chopped fresh chives

*1/4 cup Roasted Garlic (see Appendices),
puréed*

3 cups chanterelle mushrooms, cleaned

1 shallot, minced

4 squab breasts, boned

*1/2 cup Squab Reduction, hot
(see Appendices)*

*1/4 cup Red Wine Reduction, hot
(see Appendices)*

4 teaspoons long-cut fresh chives

METHOD To prepare the squab legs: Season the legs with salt and pepper. Sear with 2 teaspoons grapeseed oil in a hot saucepan over medium heat for 2 minutes on each side. Remove the squab legs and add the carrot, leek, chopped onion, and celery to the pan. Cook over medium-high heat for 3 minutes, or until golden brown. Add the tomato paste and deglaze with the red wine. Return the squab legs to the pan, add the garlic, and cover with 2 cups of the Chicken Stock. Bring to a slow simmer over medium-low heat, cover with a tight-fitting lid, and cook for 2 hours, or until very tender. (The braising liquid can be strained, reduced, and used as a sauce.)

To prepare the risotto: Place the julienned onion and 2 tablespoons of the butter in a medium sauté pan and cook over medium heat for 10 to 15 minutes, or until golden brown. Remove the onion from the heat and set aside. Cook the minced garlic and minced onion with 2 tablespoons of the butter in a large sauté pan over medium heat for 3 minutes, or until the onion is translucent. Add the rice and cook for 2 minutes, stirring frequently. Slowly add 1/4 cup of the Chicken Stock and stir until it is completely absorbed. Add 2 3/4 cups of the Chicken Stock, 1/4 cup at a time, stirring continuously with a smooth, gentle motion until the liquid is completely absorbed before adding more. (The risotto will take 40 to 50 minutes to cook completely.) Fold in the caramelized onion, chopped chives, and Roasted Garlic and season to taste with salt and pepper.

To prepare the mushrooms: Sauté the mushrooms with the shallot and the remaining 2 tablespoons butter in a sauté pan over medium-high heat for 3 minutes, or until tender. Season to taste with salt and pepper. Purée one-third of the mushrooms with the remaining 1/2 cup Chicken Stock until smooth.

To prepare the squab breasts: Season the breasts with salt and pepper. Place the breasts, skin side down, in a hot sauté pan with the remaining 1 tablespoon grapeseed oil and cook for 4 minutes on each side, or until cooked medium-rare. Let rest for 3 minutes, cut the breasts into 1/4-inch-thick slices, and season to taste with salt and pepper.

ASSEMBLY Place some of the risotto in the center of each plate. Arrange the mushrooms in front of the risotto and lean a squab leg next to the mushrooms. Arrange the squab breast meat in front of the leg. Spoon the mushroom purée around the plate, making a square. Spoon the Squab Stock Reduction and Red Wine Reduction around the plate. Sprinkle with the long-cut chives and top with freshly ground black pepper.

Substitutions

Chicken, beef, veal

Wine Notes

For sweet roasted garlic, caramelized onion, and dark rich squab meat, only a red wine will do. Sangiovese with an earthy component and good acidity will ground the dish. Fine Sangiovese-dominated Chiantis from producers who value dense structure and concentration, like Isole e Olena and Antinori in *Pepoli*, will shine.

Squab with Hijiki Seaweed Sauce, Matsutake Mushrooms, and Fennel Seed

~~~~~~

The fennel seed–flavored squab breast is nicely offset by the delicate, almost straw-flavored matsutake mushroom pieces. Additionally, a purée of the mushrooms comes across as a "cream" reinforcement of that haunting flavor. An earthy, musty meat juice flavored with hijiki seaweed and sesame oil adds a masculine balance, and small turnip pieces provide just the right playful bite.

Serves 4

1 cup dried hijiki seaweed, soaked in water overnight

1 1/2 cups Meat Stock Reduction (see Appendices)

1 tablespoon sesame oil

1 tablespoon mirin

2 teaspoons tamari soy sauce

1 cup thinly sliced matsutake mushrooms

2 tablespoons butter

Salt and pepper

1 cup Roasted Matsutake Mushrooms (see Appendices)

1/4 cup water

8 baby turnips, peeled and tops trimmed

2 squabs, trussed

2 tablespoons grapeseed oil

2 tablespoons fennel seeds

1 teaspoon fresh thyme leaves

METHOD To prepare the seaweed sauce: Drain the hijiki. Measure out 1/4 cup of the hijiki and set aside. Purée the remaining hijiki with the Meat Stock Reduction, sesame oil, mirin, and tamari. Pass through a fine-mesh sieve and warm in a small saucepan just prior to serving.

To prepare the mushrooms: Sauté the sliced mushrooms in 1 tablespoon of the butter in a sauté pan over medium heat for 2 minutes, or until tender. Season to taste with salt and pepper.

Combine the roasted mushrooms with the water and any juices that remain from roasting and purée until smooth. Season to taste with salt and pepper. Warm in a small saucepan just prior to serving.

To prepare the turnips: Place the turnips in a sauté pan with 1 tablespoon of the butter and cook over medium heat for 10 minutes, or until caramelized. Season to taste with salt and pepper.

To prepare the squabs: Preheat the oven to 400 degrees. Season the squabs with salt and pepper. Sear the squabs with the grapeseed oil in a hot sauté pan over medium-high heat for 2 minutes on each side, or until golden brown. Sprinkle with the fennel seeds and roast for 10 minutes, or until cooked medium. Remove from the oven and let rest for 3 minutes. Remove the breasts from the bone and cut each breast in half. Season to taste with salt and pepper. (Reserve the remaining parts of the squabs for another use.)

ASSEMBLY Spoon the matsutake mushroom purée in a large triangle in the center of each plate. Spoon the seaweed sauce in a large triangle just overlapping the mushroom purée. Arrange the mushroom slices over the sauces, and place 2 pieces of squab breast in the center of the plate. Sprinkle the reserved hijiki seaweed and thyme leaves around the plate and top with freshly ground black pepper.

Substitutions

Beef, lamb, chicken

Wine Notes

Pine-scented matsutake mushrooms find a friend in Cabernet Franc. The black hijiki seaweed and rich, nutty sesame oil mandate a deeply textured style with low acidity. A luxurious option is a younger right bank Bordeaux from St. Émilion called Chateau Cheval Blanc, which has a characteristic spicy richness and velvety texture. More accessible are New World translations from La Jota and Beringer in California that retain the woodsy, herbaceous character of the grape.

Smoked Squab Breast with Israeli Couscous–Stuffed Tinker Bell Peppers, Ennis Hazelnuts, and Savory Chocolate Vinaigrette

Chocolate works superbly with full-flavored meats such as squab or venison. It has a musty earthiness that completely anchors the luscious fullness of the meat. Here, sweet, rich hazelnuts add even greater depth of flavor, and the orange-honey crust on the squab delivers a profound sweet-bitter accent. Small sweet peppers stuffed with a toothsome couscous provide both playfulness and refined substance. The sauce can easily be made spicy by blending in some roasted chiles.

Serves 4

4 squab breasts, boned

Salt and pepper

3 cups hickory wood chips, soaked in water for 1 hour

4 Tinker Bell peppers

1 teaspoon grapeseed oil

1/2 cup cooked Israeli couscous

1 tablespoon olive oil

2 scallions, blanched and finely chopped

1/4 cup cooked small-diced bacon

1 teaspoon chopped fresh tarragon

4 oranges

1 teaspoon cocoa powder

1/4 cup hazelnut oil

1 cup julienned red onion

2 tablespoons butter

1/4 cup Ennis hazelnuts, toasted, skinned, and halved

2 tablespoons julienned orange zest

2 teaspoons coriander seeds, ground

2 tablespoons honey

1 cup loosely packed mâche

METHOD To prepare the squab breasts: Season the breasts with salt and pepper and place the breasts in a smoker or a grill with the hickory chips. Smoke over medium heat for 10 minutes, or until cooked medium-rare. If necessary, warm the squab in the oven just prior to serving.

To prepare the peppers: Rub the Tinker Bell peppers with the grapeseed oil and roast over an open flame or in the broiler for 1 minute on each side, or until the outside is charred. Place in a bowl, cover with plastic wrap, and let steam for 5 minutes. Carefully remove the charred skin from the peppers. Cut off and reserve the tops and remove the seeds from the peppers.

Toss the Israeli couscous with the olive oil, scallions, and bacon and season to taste with salt and pepper. Fill the peppers with the couscous mixture and cover with the reserved tops. Sprinkle the stuffed peppers with the tarragon. If necessary, warm the stuffed peppers in the oven just prior to serving.

To prepare the vinaigrette: Juice the oranges and place the juice in a small saucepan. Cook over medium heat for 10 to 15 minutes, or until reduced to 1/4 cup. Add the cocoa powder and whisk in the hazelnut oil. Season to taste with salt and pepper.

To prepare the onion: Place the red onion and 1 tablespoon of the butter in a small sauté pan and cook over medium heat for 4 to 5 minutes, or until caramelized. Season to taste with salt and pepper.

To prepare the hazelnuts: Place the hazelnuts and the remaining 1 tablespoon butter in a small sauté pan. Cook over high heat for 1 minute, or until the hazelnuts are caramelized.

To prepare the crust: Blanch the orange zest in boiling water. Purée the orange zest with the coriander and honey. Spread a thin layer of the orange purée over the smoked squab breasts. Thinly slice the squab breasts and season with salt and pepper.

ASSEMBLY Arrange some of the caramelized onion in a long line at an angle across the center of each plate. Place the squab slices over the onion. Place a stuffed pepper to the left of the squab. Spoon the chocolate vinaigrette around the plate. Sprinkle the hazelnuts and mâche around the plate and top with freshly ground black pepper.

Substitutions

Chicken, poussin, bass

Wine Notes

In this dish, the sweet, earthy flavors of caramelized onion, smoky meat, and decadent chocolate sauce are tempered with citrus. The high notes are the orange zest on the squab and the orange juice in the sauce. Similarly, the wine for this course should preserve the brightness while displaying a restrained richness. Whereas south Australian Shiraz is sometimes over the top with jammy, ripe fruit, when planted in a temperate climate like the Yarra Valley in Victoria, the results are different. Yarra Yerring *Dry Red No. 2* is a Shiraz-based blend with the necessary elegant balance.

Grouse Breast with Red Wine–Braised Prunes, Gingered Chard, Cinnamon Cap Mushrooms, and Sage

Grouse, which is fairly full flavored and rich, needs to be balanced with assertive flavors. Prunes are ideal, being plump, sweet, and jammy, and here they take on added complexity with a slow braise in red wine. Additionally, chard, cooked down and flavored with ginger, makes the preparation even more spectacular. Cinnamon cap mushrooms provide an important earthiness, and sage and chard sprouts add the perfect touch of whimsy.

Serves 4

12 prunes, pitted

1/2 cup Red Wine Reduction (see Appendices)

1 cup Beef Stock Reduction (see Appendices)

3 tablespoons Preserved Ginger (see Appendices)

2 shallots, minced

3 cloves garlic, minced

3 tablespoons butter

1 tablespoon minced fresh ginger

8 leaves Swiss chard, stems removed and chopped

2 cups Vegetable Stock (see Appendices)

Salt and pepper

4 grouse breasts, boned

4 grouse legs

4 teaspoons grapeseed oil

4 teaspoons finely julienned fresh sage leaves

1 1/2 cups Roasted Tiny Cinnamon Cap Mushrooms (see Appendices)

1/4 cup loosely packed baby rainbow chard sprouts

METHOD To prepare the prunes: Place the prunes, Red Wine Reduction, and Beef Stock Reduction in a small saucepan and simmer over low heat for 30 to 40 minutes, or until the prunes are tender. Leave the prunes in the braising liquid until ready to serve, then reserve the braising liquid for a sauce.

To prepare the gingered chard: Finely chop the Preserved Ginger. Sweat the shallots and garlic with the butter in a medium sauté pan over medium heat for 1 minute. Add the fresh ginger and Swiss chard and cook for 1 minute. Add the Vegetable Stock and cook over low heat for 20 to 30 minutes, or until the chard is very tender. Season to taste with salt and pepper. Drain the chard, reserving the cooking liquid. Finely chop the chard.

To prepare the grouse: Season the grouse breasts and legs with salt and pepper. Place the grouse pieces in a hot sauté pan with the grapeseed oil and cook over medium heat for 2 1/2 minutes on each side, or until cooked medium. Remove the grouse from pan and let rest for 2 minutes. Cut the breasts into 5 slices and season with salt and pepper. Reserve the grouse legs whole.

ASSEMBLY Arrange 3 of the braised prunes in the center of each plate and sprinkle with the sage. Spoon the gingered chard in a ring around the plate. Place the grouse leg at the top of the plate and arrange the breast slices at 5 points around the plate. Arrange the mushrooms around the plate and spoon on the braising liquid from the prunes and the chard. Sprinkle with the chard sprouts and top with freshly ground black pepper.

Substitutions

Squab, beef, chicken

Wine Notes

A full-bodied red comes to mind to accompany this presentation. South Australian Shiraz, particularly Barossa Valley, with its facets of spice and stewed ripe fruit, can diminish the gamy quality of the grouse while paralleling the Preserved Ginger flavors and the sweetness of the prunes. Try the *Command* Shiraz from Elderton.

Deconstructed Lamb Tenderloin Salad
with Matsutake Mushrooms, Green Tea Noodles,
Tofu, and Mirin-Scallion Purée

*This is a fairly light and refreshing salad with lots of wonderful textures and flavors. By breaking
the components apart, one can appreciate the flavor characteristics of each ingredient. Additionally,
reducing or increasing the amount of each element can help tailor this dish for a specific menu.
The mirin-scallion purée provides the perfect sweet-sharp note to the lamb, mushrooms, and noodles,
and the soy sauce adds a welcome saltiness that helps harmonize the remaining elements.*

Serves 4

4¹/₂ tablespoons sesame oil

2 tablespoons freshly squeezed orange juice

1 tablespoon chopped fresh ginger

1 tablespoon chopped lemongrass

1 8-ounce lamb tenderloin

2 teaspoons white sesame seeds, toasted

1¹/₂ teaspoons black sesame seeds, toasted

Salt and pepper

4 scallions, blanched and chopped

3 tablespoons mirin

¹/₂ cup cold water

2 heads baby bok choy

2 teaspoons grapeseed oil

1 clove garlic, thinly sliced

*3 large matsutake mushrooms, cleaned and
thinly sliced*

3 tablespoons tamari soy sauce

¹/₂ cup peeled, julienned apple

2 radishes, julienned

3 tablespoons freshly squeezed lemon juice

1 cup medium-diced firm tofu

2 tablespoons fresh cilantro chiffonade

2 ounces green tea noodles, cooked

¹/₄ cup loosely packed micro tatsoi

¹/₄ cup roasted soybeans

METHOD To prepare the lamb: Mix together 2 tablespoons of the sesame oil, the orange juice, 2 teaspoons of the ginger, and the lemongrass in a large bowl. Rub over the lamb and refrigerate for 1 hour.

Remove the lamb from the marinade and place it in a hot sauté pan. Cook over medium-high heat for 2 minutes on each side, or until cooked rare. Allow the lamb to cool to room temperature. Roll the cooked lamb in 1¹/₂ teaspoons of the white sesame seeds and all of the black sesame seeds. Cut the lamb into 20 equal slices and season to taste with salt and pepper.

To make the scallion purée: Purée the scallions with 2 tablespoons of the mirin and ¹/₄ cup of the water until smooth. Season to taste with salt and pepper.

To prepare the bok choy: Cook the bok choy, the grapeseed oil, the remaining 1 teaspoon ginger, the remaining ¹/₄ cup water, and the garlic in a medium sauté pan over medium heat for 2 to 3 minutes, or until tender. Season to taste with salt and pepper.

To prepare the mushrooms: Toss the matsutake mushrooms with 2 tablespoons of the tamari, the remaining 1 tablespoon mirin, and 1 tablespoon of the sesame oil in a small bowl. Season to taste with salt and pepper.

To prepare the apple mixture: Toss the apple and radishes with 1 tablespoon of the lemon juice in a small bowl. Season to taste with salt and pepper. Toss the tofu with the remaining 2 tablespoons lemon juice and the cilantro in a small bowl. Season to taste with salt and pepper.

To prepare the noodles: Toss the noodles with 2 tablespoons of the micro tatsoi and the remaining ¹/₂ teaspoon white sesame seeds, 1¹/₂ tablespoons sesame oil, and the remaining 1 tablespoon tamari in a large bowl. Season to taste with salt and pepper.

ASSEMBLY Place some of the noodles at the top of each plate and continue moving around the plate with the apple mixture, lamb slices, bok choy, and mushrooms. Place the tofu in the center of the plate and spoon the scallion purée around the plate. Drizzle the marinating juices from the mushrooms around the plate and sprinkle with the remaining 2 tablespoons micro tatsoi sprouts and the roasted soybeans.

Substitutions

Chicken, beef, veal

Wine Notes

The prominent Asian leanings of this salad lead one to the neoclassic pairing of Asian foods with sparkling wine. New World sparkling wine, in particular the *Vrais Amis* cuvée from Iron Horse in Green Valley, Sonoma, with its Pinot Noir dominance, provides the necessary fruit component to balance the nutty elements—toasted sesame seeds and sesame oil—with the green elements—cilantro and bok choy.

French Onion Soup with Shredded Pork, Goat's Milk Brie, and Sourdough Croutons

This play on a classic French onion soup promotes heartier and more poignant flavors.
Shredded Pork adds a deeply satisfying richness, and the meltingly soft goat brie simultaneously provides
creaminess and tanginess. By using sourdough bread for the croutons, a pleasant complexity
is achieved. Although they don't appear here, black truffles would push this whole dish over the top.

Serves 4

6 Vidalia onions, julienned

1/4 cup butter

Salt and pepper

3/4 cup sherry

9 cups Beef Consommé (see Appendices)

32 1 by 1/4-inch round slices sourdough bread

8 ounces Shredded Pork (recipe follows)

*4 ounces goat's milk brie, cut into
16 thin slices*

1 tablespoon chopped fresh chives

1 tablespoon fresh thyme leaves

METHOD To prepare the soup: Sweat the onions with the butter in a large saucepan over medium-low heat for 30 minutes, or until golden brown. Season to taste with salt and pepper. Deglaze with the sherry and cook for 2 minutes. Add the Beef Consommé, simmer for 15 minutes, and season to taste with salt and pepper.

To prepare the croutons: Preheat the oven to 350 degrees. Toast the sourdough bread in the oven for 10 to 12 minutes, or until golden brown. Divide the Shredded Pork evenly among half of the croutons, and place a slice of brie on each of the remaining croutons.

ASSEMBLY Ladle some of the soup into each shallow bowl. Arrange 4 of each type of crouton in each bowl. Sprinkle with the chives and thyme and top with freshly ground black pepper.

Shredded Pork

Yield: 1 pound

1 pound pork butt

1 cup kosher salt

1 cup firmly packed brown sugar

1 sprig rosemary, leaves picked

2 sprigs thyme

1 tablespoon mustard seeds

1 1/2 teaspoons coriander seeds

2 star anise

1 whole clove

1/2 teaspoon ground cinnamon

1 1/2 teaspoons fennel seeds

2 quarts water

1 cup chopped Spanish onion

1 cup chopped carrot

1 cup chopped leek

1 cup chopped celery

1 tablespoon grapeseed oil

1 bay leaf

1 teaspoon peppercorns

2 jalapeño chiles, seeded and chopped

5 cloves garlic

1 quart Beef Stock (see Appendices)

Salt and pepper

METHOD Prepare an ice-water bath. Using a fork, poke holes in the pork. Place the salt and brown sugar in a medium saucepan. Place the rosemary, thyme, mustard seeds, coriander seeds, star anise, clove, cinnamon, and fennel seeds in a hot sauté pan and roast over medium heat for 2 minutes. Add the roasted spices and water to the saucepan and bring to a simmer over medium heat. Cook for 5 minutes, or until the sugar and salt are dissolved. Cool over the ice-water bath. Place the pork in a deep container and pour in the cooled cure. Refrigerate overnight.

Remove the pork from the cure. Preheat the oven to 250 degrees. Cook the onion, carrot, leek, and celery in a large braising pan with the grapeseed oil over medium-high heat for 3 to 5 minutes, or until golden brown. Add the pork, bay leaf, peppercorns, jalapeño, garlic, and Beef Stock. Bring the mixture to a simmer over medium heat and cover. Braise in the oven for 6 to 8 hours, or until the meat is fork tender. Cool the pork in the liquid.

Remove the pork from the liquid and shred the meat with a fork. Season to taste with salt and pepper. Reserve 2 cups of the braising liquid in which to reheat the shredded pork, if necessary.

Substitutions

Beef, oxtail, veal

Wine Notes

The earthy sweetness from the caramelized onions and shredded pork and the richness from the brie ask for a big wine tempered with good acidity. While the soup might pair well with an Alsatian Riesling or a Vouvray Sec, a more compelling answer is a full-bodied Riesling Smaragd from the Wachau in Austria. Nigl's Kremser Kremsleiten is a lush, well-balanced dry Riesling whose flavors marry with the brown spiced pork and have the acidity to stand up to the brie.

Lamb Shank Tortellini with Oven-Roasted Tomatoes, Saffron Emulsion, Thyme, and Sage

Another great way to enjoy a lamb shank is to shred the meat and encase it in pasta. The resulting "pouch" is delicate but hearty. Here, a saffron emulsion provides an ethereal but poignant note, and the earthy roasted tomato pieces add just the right acidic sweetness to temper the succulent meat.

Serves 4

1 Braised Lamb Shank (see Appendices)

1 shallot, minced

1 tablespoon olive oil

12 Roasted Garlic cloves, cut into quarters (see Appendices)

2 tablespoons chopped fresh chives

1 tablespoon balsamic vinegar

Salt and pepper

Sage Pasta (see Appendices)

1 egg, lightly beaten

1½ cups fresh tomato juice

1½ cups Vegetable Stock (see Appendices)

Pinch of saffron threads

¼ cup butter

2 teaspoons rice vinegar

Oven-Roasted Tomatoes (recipe follows)

4 teaspoons Rosemary Oil (see Appendices)

1 sprig rosemary, leaves picked

METHOD To prepare the lamb shank: Using a fork, pull the meat from the shank into small pieces. Sweat the shallot with the olive oil in a sauté pan over medium heat for 1 minute. Add two-thirds of the Roasted Garlic pieces, the chives, and the balsamic vinegar and fold the mixture into the lamb shank meat. Season to taste with salt and pepper.

To prepare the tortellini: Cut the pasta into 16 4-inch squares. Place 1 tablespoon of the lamb shank mixture in the center of a square. Lightly brush the outside edges of the square with the egg wash. Fold the square into a triangle and gently press the edges together. Bring the 2 far corners together and moisten 1 corner with the beaten egg to seal them together. As the tortellini are made, place them on a lightly floured sheet pan. Refrigerate until ready to cook.

Just prior to serving, cook the tortellini in boiling salted water for 3 minutes, or until al dente. Remove from the water with a slotted spoon and drain well.

To prepare the tomato reduction: Place the tomato juice in a small saucepan and cook over low heat, skimming occasionally, for 1 hour, or until reduced to about ⅓ cup.

To prepare the saffron emulsion: Place the Vegetable Stock and saffron in a small saucepan and simmer over medium heat for 3 minutes. Whisk in the butter and rice vinegar and season to taste with salt and pepper. Froth with a handheld blender just prior to serving.

ASSEMBLY Place 2 tortellini upright in the center of each plate. Arrange some of the tomato pieces and roasted garlic pieces around the tortellini. Spoon some of the saffron emulsion over the tortellini and around the plate. Spoon some of the tomato reduction and Rosemary Oil around the plate. Sprinkle with the rosemary leaves.

Oven-Roasted Tomatoes

Yield: 1 cup

3 plum tomatoes, halved lengthwise

5 tablespoons olive oil

Salt and pepper

15 sprigs thyme

2 teaspoons balsamic vinegar

METHOD Preheat the oven to 225 degrees. Rub the cut side of the tomatoes with 4 tablespoons of the olive oil and season with salt and pepper. Place cut side up on a small sheet pan lined with a wire rack and lay the thyme sprigs over the tomatoes. Roast in the oven for 3 hours, or until the tomatoes are dehydrated by about half but not dry. Remove and discard the skin and seeds from the tomatoes. Cut each half into quarters.

Just prior to serving, toss the tomatoes with the remaining 1 tablespoon olive oil and the balsamic vinegar and season to taste with salt and pepper. Warm in the oven if necessary.

Substitutions

Beef, veal, oxtail

Wine Notes

New World Sauvignon Blanc, particularly those from Marlborough, on the northern tip of the southern island of New Zealand, tend to show a zippy, green acidity. With producers like Giesen, the wine can also exhibit a tomato-leaf character that marries well with the saffron and roasted tomatoes in this dish, while the acidity cuts nicely through the richness of the lamb.

Veal Loin Cooked in a Salt Crust with Morels, Asparagus, Golden Beets, and Parsley Purée

Arguably, the most succulent way to enjoy veal loin is to cook it slowly in a salt crust.
Done properly, the result is perfectly cooked, pink, soft, buttery meat. Here, slices of the meat are paired
with morel mushrooms, asparagus, and tiny golden beets. Parsley and rosemary flavor
the dish, and all the elements come together in fabulous harmony, with the veal taking the lead.

Serves 4

12 baby golden beets

½ cup plus 1 tablespoon olive oil

Salt and pepper

1 cup loosely packed fresh flat-leaf parsley leaves

4 egg whites

2 cups rock salt

4 sprigs rosemary

4 sprigs thyme

4 sprigs flat-leaf parsley

1 1-pound veal tenderloin (not more than 2 inches in diameter)

2 cups morel mushrooms, cleaned

1 shallot, cut into thin rings

3 tablespoons butter

⅓ cup Chicken Stock (see Appendices)

16 thin asparagus spears

1 tablespoon minced shallot

½ cup Veal Stock Reduction, hot (see Appendices)

8 teaspoons Rosemary Oil (see Appendices)

Fleur de sel

2 teaspoons fresh rosemary leaves

METHOD To prepare the beets: Preheat the oven to 400 degrees. Rub the beets with 1 tablespoon of the olive oil and season with salt and pepper. Place in an ovenproof pan and roast in the oven for 1 hour, or until tender. Peel the beets, slice into thin disks, and season to taste with salt and pepper.

To prepare the parsley purée: Quickly sauté the parsley leaves in 2 tablespoons of the olive oil over high heat for 2 minutes, or until wilted. Place the pan in the freezer for 10 minutes. Purée the parsley with the remaining 6 tablespoons olive oil. Place the purée in a small saucepan, season to taste with salt and pepper, and warm just prior to serving.

To prepare the veal: Preheat the oven to 425 degrees. Whip the egg whites in an electric mixer until stiff peaks form. Fold in the rock salt and spread half of the mixture on a sheet pan. Lay half of the rosemary, thyme, and parsley sprigs over the egg white mixture. Place the veal tenderloin over the herbs and cover with the remaining herbs and egg white mixture. Bake for 25 minutes, or to an internal temperature of 140 degrees. Remove the salt crust from the veal and brush off the herbs. Cut the veal tenderloin into 24 equal slices, and season to taste with salt and pepper.

To prepare the morels: Sauté the morels and shallot rings with 1 tablespoon of the butter in a medium sauté pan over medium heat for 2 minutes. Add the Chicken Stock and season to taste with salt and pepper. Cook for 2 minutes, or until the morels are tender. Keep warm until ready to serve.

To prepare the asparagus: Cut the asparagus spears in half. Sauté the asparagus with the minced shallot and the remaining 2 tablespoons butter in a sauté pan over medium heat for 5 to 7 minutes, or until tender.

ASSEMBLY Arrange one-fourth of the beet slices, morel mushrooms, and asparagus in the center of each plate. Place 6 veal slices over the vegetables. Spoon the reserved cooking juices from the mushrooms around the plate along with the Veal Stock Reduction, parsley purée, and Rosemary Oil. Sprinkle the fleur de sel and rosemary leaves over the veal.

Substitutions

Beef, chicken, pork

Wine Notes

Tender, salty veal is lent an earthy sweetness by the beets and a richness by the morels. In the chalky vineyards of Pouilly-Fumé, the Sauvignon Blanc is crisp, clean, and very aromatic. A racy Pouilly-Fumé such as Didier Dageneau's *En Chailloux* adds a crisp spark to the dish that counters the salt and also complements the herbs.

...Man is the only animal that can remain on friendly terms wit

e victims he intends to eat until he eats them.—SAMUEL BUTLER

Cumin-and-Coriander-Scented Lamb Tenderloin with Green Olives, English Peas, and Cucumber-Yogurt Sauce

This preparation is light and delicate, yet distinctly flavored with the spices and olive pieces.
The tangy, creamy yogurt sauce acts as the perfect backdrop to the complex Mediterranean flavors.
English peas flavored with mint and globe basil round out the dish with floral notes.
Finally, a drizzle of lamb jus pushes the various refined flavor notes into slightly heartier territory.

Serves 4

¼ teaspoon ground cinnamon

¼ teaspoon ground cardamom

¼ teaspoon pepper

¼ teaspoon ground cumin

¼ teaspoon ground coriander

¼ teaspoon kosher salt

1 8-ounce lamb tenderloin

2 teaspoons grapeseed oil

Salt and pepper

½ cup plain yogurt

½ cup peeled, seeded, and chopped cucumber

1 tablespoon plus ¼ teaspoon freshly squeezed lime juice

8 green olives, pitted

¼ cup Basil Oil (see Appendices)

1 cup peeled, seeded, and finely julienned cucumber

¼ cup loosely packed fresh globe basil leaves

16 tangerine sections

½ cup shelled English peas, blanched and shocked

¼ cup Mint Oil (recipe follows)

METHOD To prepare the lamb: Combine the cinnamon, cardamom, ¼ teaspoon pepper, cumin, coriander, and kosher salt in a small bowl. Season the outside of the lamb loin with the spice rub and refrigerate for 1 hour.

Sauté the lamb with the grapeseed oil in a hot sauté pan over medium-high heat for 4 to 5 minutes on each side, or until cooked medium-rare. Remove the lamb from the pan. Just prior to serving, cut the loin into 16 equal slices and season to taste with salt and pepper. Reserve any juices from slicing the lamb.

To prepare the sauce: Purée the yogurt, chopped cucumber, and 1 tablespoon of the lime juice until smooth. Season to taste with salt and pepper.

To prepare the olives: Marinate the olives in the Basil Oil for at least 1 hour. Remove from the oil and cut the olives into eighths.

To prepare the cucumber: Toss the julienned cucumber with the remaining ¼ teaspoon lime juice and half of the globe basil. Season to taste with salt and pepper.

ASSEMBLY Place a mound of the cucumbers in the center of each plate and alternate the lamb slices and tangerine sections around the cucumber. Spoon the yogurt sauce around the plate along with the reserved lamb juices. Toss the peas with the Mint Oil, season to taste with salt and pepper, and spoon around the plate. Sprinkle the olive slices and the remaining globe basil around the plate. Top with freshly ground black pepper.

Mint Oil

Yield: ½ cup

½ cup firmly packed fresh mint leaves

1 cup firmly packed spinach

½ cup plus 1 tablespoon grapeseed oil

¼ cup olive oil

METHOD Sauté the mint leaves and spinach with 1 tablespoon of the grapeseed oil in a small sauté pan over medium heat for 2 minutes, or until wilted. Immediately shock in ice water and drain. Coarsely chop the mixture and squeeze out the excess water. Purée the spinach mixture with the remaining ½ cup grapeseed oil and the olive oil for 3 to 4 minutes, or until bright green. Pour into a container, cover, and refrigerate for 1 day.

Strain through a fine-mesh sieve and discard the solids. Refrigerate for 1 day, decant, and refrigerate until ready to use or for up to 2 weeks.

Substitutions

Beef, veal, salmon

Wine Notes

The delicate acidity present in the cucumbers and sweet English peas, and the vibrant citrus in the lime and tangerine come together to give this dish a cool and refreshing character. Viognier, prized for its tantalizing perfumes of violets, peaches, and apricots, makes a brilliant partner. Morgan Clendenen, a Viognier specialist from the Central Coast of California, produces Cold Heaven's Edna Valley Viognier, which displays an elegant richness that stands up to the spiced lamb and preserves the freshness of the dish.

Rabbit-Polenta Terrine with Truffled Mascarpone, Black Trumpet Mushrooms, and Chervil

This earthy dish is dressed up with a dollop of truffled mascarpone.
Smearing it into the other elements with each bite offers an utterly sublime taste sensation.
Meat juice could be drizzled around if a richer preparation is desired.

Serves 12

8 rabbit tenderloins (about 12 ounces total)

Salt and pepper

2 tablespoons grapeseed oil

1/2 cup chopped black truffle

2 large Swiss chard leaves, stems removed and blanched

1/2 cup plus 2 tablespoons olive oil

2 tablespoons chopped fresh chervil

1 1/2 cups cooked polenta, warm

3 cups Roasted Black Trumpet Mushrooms (see Appendices)

2 tablespoons sherry wine vinegar

1/4 cup white truffle oil

1 cup mascarpone cheese

1/2 cup heavy whipping cream

1/4 cup loosely packed micro chervil sprouts

METHOD To prepare the rabbit: Season the rabbit tenderloins with salt and pepper. Cook the rabbit with the grapeseed oil in a hot sauté pan over medium-high heat for 2 minutes on each side, or until just cooked. Sprinkle 2 loins with some of the black truffle and wrap in the Swiss chard. Trim the edges straight and set aside.

To assemble the terrine: Line an 8 by 2 1/4 by 1 1/2-inch terrine mold with plastic wrap, allowing some to drape over the sides. Fold 2 tablespoons of the olive oil and the chervil into the polenta and season to taste with salt and pepper. Spoon some of the polenta mixture into the mold, filling it one-third full. Lay the 2 wrapped rabbit loins in the polenta, running them the length of the terrine. (The loins may need to be cut to fit exactly.) Spoon enough of the remaining polenta over the rabbit to fill the mold. Firmly press down on the terrine with your fingers or a small wooden board. Fold the excess plastic wrap over the terrine and refrigerate for 1 hour, or until set.

Preheat the oven to 350 degrees. Remove the terrine from the mold and rewrap tightly in a piece of plastic wrap. Using a very sharp knife, cut the terrine into 12 slices each about 1/2 inch thick. Remove the plastic wrap from each piece. Warm the terrine slices in the oven for 5 minutes, or until warm.

To prepare the vinaigrette: Cut the black trumpet mushrooms into small bite-sized pieces and place in a medium bowl. Add the sherry wine vinegar and whisk in the truffle oil and the remaining 1/2 cup olive oil. Season to taste with salt and pepper.

To prepare the mascarpone cream: Place the mascarpone and cream in a small bowl. Whip until medium-stiff peaks begin to form. Fold in the remaining black truffle and season to taste with salt and pepper. Refrigerate until ready to serve.

ASSEMBLY Place a slice of the terrine in the center of each plate. Place a "quenelle" of the mascarpone cream at one side of the plate, and spoon some of the black trumpet vinaigrette around the plate. Slice the remaining rabbit loins into 1/2-inch-thick pieces on the diagonal. Place 3 pieces of the rabbit around the terrine slice. Sprinkle with the chervil sprouts and top with freshly ground black pepper.

Substitutions

Chicken, pork, pheasant

Wine Notes

Rich, perfumed truffles and earthy notes from the black trumpet mushrooms speak to the white wines of Burgundy. *Terroir*-oriented wines, such as traditionalist Francois Jobard's Meursault-Poruzots with their smoky, almost oxidative character, add a hedonistically rich layer to the dish.

Soup of Braised Oxtail and Morel Mushrooms with Leek Emulsion

*Although it is undeniably earthy and luscious, this preparation is also quite light.
The clean, woodsy, subtly powerful flavor of the morel mushroom soup is the ideal canvas for the soulful,
succulent Braised Oxtail. Whole morels and pieces of buttery braised leek provide a wonderful
textural contrast for the meat. A satiny leek emulsion adds a pleasant richness, and micro celery sprouts provide
a vital cleansing spark. The flavors and textures here are simple and at the same time complex.*

Serves 4

4 cups morel mushrooms, cleaned

2 tablespoons minced shallot

2 cloves garlic, minced

½ cup plus 2 tablespoons butter

Salt and pepper

3 cups Mushroom Stock (see Appendices)

3 cups Chicken Stock (see Appendices)

2 large leeks (white part only)

1 cup warm Braised Oxtail (see Appendices)

2 tablespoons micro celery sprouts

METHOD To prepare the mushrooms: Sauté the mushrooms with the shallot, garlic, and 2 tablespoons of the butter in a large sauté pan over medium heat for 5 to 7 minutes, or until tender. Season to taste with salt and pepper. Purée half of the mushrooms with all of the Mushroom Stock and 1 cup of the Chicken Stock until smooth. Pass through a fine-mesh sieve and season to taste with salt and pepper. Warm just prior to serving.

To prepare the leeks: Truss the leeks with butcher's twine to keep them together while braising. Place the leeks and ¼ cup of the butter in a medium sauté pan and cover with the remaining 2 cups Chicken Stock. Slowly simmer the leeks over medium low heat for 30 minutes, or until tender.

Remove the leeks, reserving the cooking liquid, and cut away the twine. Slice 1 of the leeks on the diagonal and coarsely chop the remaining leek. Purée the chopped leek with the cooking liquid and pass through a fine-mesh sieve. Place the purée in a saucepan, warm over medium heat, and season to taste with salt and pepper. Whisk in the remaining ¼ cup butter and froth with a handheld blender just prior to serving.

ASSEMBLY Ladle some of the hot soup into each shallow bowl. Arrange the mushrooms, Braised Oxtail, and leek slices around the bowl. Spoon the leek emulsion around the outer rim of the bowl. Sprinkle the micro celery sprouts around the bowl and top with freshly ground black pepper.

Substitutions

Beef, veal, pork, scallops

Wine Notes

A smartly styled Chardonnay from California, like David Ramey's *Hyde Vineyard* from the Napa side of Carneros, provides a nice cushion for the buttery, foamy leek emulsion and for the hot morel soup. The oxtail is also well met by the firm structure and spice of the wine. Many other stylistically similar Chardonnays, such as those from Saintsbury, Patz and Hall, and Kistler, would also be a satisfying fit.

Rabbit Loin with English Pea Risotto, Black Trumpet Mushrooms and Their Purée, and Globe Basil

The delicate, clean flavor and buttery texture of rabbit loin could not have two better friends than English peas and black trumpet mushrooms. The peas, with their irresistible sweetness and refined starchiness, help to coax out the rabbit's milky flavor, while the soft, majestic, woodsy flavor of the black trumpets serves as a necessary contrast. Here, the peas are incorporated into a risotto, so there is a substance to the dish as well. The mushrooms also feature their purée, which provides a soothing mouthfeel. A drizzle of Game Bird Stock Reduction gives additional richness, and globe basil leaves provide a playfulness.

Serves 4

1 bunch flat-leaf parsley

6 tablespoons canola oil

2 tablespoons ice water

Salt and pepper

3 shallots, minced

3 tablespoons butter

1 cup arborio rice

4 cups Chicken Stock (see Appendices)

1/3 cup grated Parmesan cheese

1 1/2 cups shelled English peas, blanched and shelled again

2 cups black trumpet mushrooms, cleaned

1/4 cup plus 1 tablespoon water

1/4 cup Basil Oil (see Appendices)

1 rabbit saddle

1 tablespoon grapeseed oil

4 teaspoons fresh basil chiffonade

2 teaspoons fresh globe basil leaves

1/4 cup Game Bird Stock Reduction, hot (see Appendices)

METHOD To prepare the purée: Sauté the parsley in 1 tablespoon of the canola oil in a hot sauté pan over medium heat for 10 seconds. Remove immediately, transfer to a small bowl, and refrigerate until cooled. Coarsely chop the parsley and purée with the ice water and the remaining 5 tablespoons canola oil until smooth. Strain through a fine-mesh sieve and season to taste with salt and pepper.

To prepare the risotto: Cook 2 of the shallots with 2 tablespoons of the butter in a large sauté pan over medium heat for 2 to 3 minutes, or until translucent. Add the rice and cook for 2 minutes, stirring frequently. Slowly add 1/4 cup of the stock and stir until completely absorbed. Add the remaining 3 3/4 cups stock, 1/4 cup at a time, stirring continuously with a smooth, gentle motion until the liquid is completely absorbed before adding more. Add the Parmesan cheese and 1 cup of the peas with the final addition of stock and season to taste with salt and pepper. (The risotto will take 40 to 50 minutes to cook completely.) Fold in the parsley purée and adjust the seasoning if necessary.

To prepare the mushrooms: Sauté the mushrooms and the remaining 1 shallot with 1 tablespoon of the butter in a medium sauté pan over medium heat for 3 to 4 minutes, or until tender. Season to taste with salt and pepper. Purée one-third of the mushroom mixture with 1/4 cup of the water and adjust the seasoning if necessary.

To prepare the peas: Place the remaining 1/2 cup peas in a small saucepan with 2 tablespoons of the Basil Oil and the remaining 1 tablespoon water and cook over medium heat for 3 minutes, or until warm. Season to taste with salt and pepper.

To prepare the rabbit: Preheat the oven to 350 degrees. Season the rabbit with salt and pepper. Sear the saddle with the grapeseed oil in a hot sauté pan over medium-high heat for 1 minute on each side. Roast the saddle in the oven for 10 minutes, or until just cooked. Allow the rabbit to rest on the bone for 3 minutes. Remove the loin from the saddle. Cut into 8 slices on the diagonal. Season to taste with salt and pepper.

ASSEMBLY Spoon some of the risotto onto the top of each plate. Arrange the mushrooms in the center of each plate and place 2 slices of the rabbit over the mushrooms. Spoon the peas around the plate, sprinkle the basil chiffonade over the risotto, and sprinkle the globe basil leaves over the rabbit. Spoon the Game Bird Stock Reduction, mushroom purée, and the remaining 2 tablespoons Basil Oil around the plate. Top with freshly ground black pepper.

Substitutions

Chicken, pork, pheasant

Wine Notes

The crunchy, sweet English peas and delicate rabbit meat keep this dish in white wine territory. The basil and black trumpet mushrooms, however, demand a more powerful white, so we turn to the Marsanne-based Hermitage of the northern Rhône Valley. Jean-Louis Chave and Marc Sorrel are top producers whose wines display rich, honeyed fruit and a great viscosity.

Asian-Glazed Wild Boar Chop with Kimchi, Burgundy Carrots, and Their Purée

Something sturdy like a boar chop stands up beautifully to the bold flavors of kimchi and togarashi. In fact, the meat seems to taste even cleaner against this dramatic backdrop than if it were paired with a heavy reduction sauce. Additionally, not only does the kimchi provide an assertive flavor, but it also delivers a welcome crunchiness. The togarashi sends out terrific heat, and the burgundy carrots and their purée complement the whole preparation with an essential sweetness.

Serves 4

8 burgundy carrots, cut into oblique wedges

2 tablespoons butter

1 bay leaf

3 sprigs thyme

½ cup Vegetable Stock (see Appendices)

Salt and pepper

1 teaspoon toasted, ground Szechuan peppercorns

1 teaspoon toasted, ground aniseeds

1 teaspoon toasted, ground fennel seeds

1 teaspoon toasted, ground coriander seeds

1 teaspoon toasted, ground green peppercorns

1 rack wild boar chops with 4 big eye chops, frenched

1 tablespoon grapeseed oil

Asian Glaze (recipe follows)

Kimchi (recipe follows)

¼ cup loosely packed pea tendrils

METHOD To prepare the carrots: Sauté the carrots with the butter in a small sauté pan over medium heat for 3 minutes. Add the bay leaf, thyme, and Vegetable Stock and cook for 3 to 4 minutes, or until tender. Remove 24 pieces of the carrot and season with salt and pepper. Purée the remaining carrots and any liquid from the pan until smooth. Season to taste with salt and pepper.

To prepare the boar chops: Preheat the oven to 350 degrees. Combine the Szechuan peppercorns, aniseeds, fennel seeds, coriander seeds, and green peppercorns in a small bowl. Season the chops with salt. Sear with the grapeseed oil in a hot sauté pan over medium-high heat for 3 minutes on each side. Brush the boar chops with some of the Asian Glaze and sprinkle with the toasted spice mixture. Roast the chops for 30 to 40 minutes, or until medium. Remove the chops from the oven and brush with some of the Asian Glaze. Let rest for 5 minutes and slice the chops apart.

ASSEMBLY Spoon some of the carrot purée in a V shape in the center of each plate. Place the Kimchi and carrot wedges in the center of the carrot purée. Place the pea tendrils over the Kimchi and place a boar chop over the tendrils. Spoon any remaining Asian Glaze around the plate and top with freshly ground black pepper.

Asian Glaze

Yield: approximately 1 cup

¼ cup finely minced Spanish onion

2 cloves garlic, minced

2 Thai chiles, seeded and minced

2 teaspoons grapeseed oil

2 tablespoons tomato paste

2 tablespoons rice vinegar

¼ cup mirin

¼ cup tamari soy sauce

2 teaspoons togarashi

¼ cup Veal Stock Reduction (see Appendices)

METHOD Sweat the onion, garlic, and Thai chiles in the grapeseed oil in a small saucepan over medium heat for 3 minutes. Add the tomato paste and cook for 2 minutes. Deglaze with the rice vinegar and mirin and stir in the tamari, togarashi, and Veal Stock Reduction.

Kimchi

Yield: 2½ to 3 cups

20 leaves napa cabbage, chopped coarsely

¼ cup kosher salt

2 cloves garlic, chopped

½ cup julienned Spanish onion

2 teaspoons grapeseed oil

2 teaspoons tomato paste

1 tablespoon chile paste

¾ cup mirin

½ cup rice vinegar

1 red Thai chile, seeded and thinly sliced

METHOD Toss the napa cabbage with the salt and place it in a casserole dish. Cover with plastic wrap and place another dish of the same size over the plastic wrap. Refrigerate for 24 hours, then rinse in cold water, and pat dry.

Sweat the garlic and onion with the grapeseed oil in a large sauté pan over medium heat for 3 to 5 minutes, or until translucent. Add the tomato paste and chile paste and cook for 3 minutes. Deglaze with the mirin and rice vinegar. Add the Thai chiles and the drained napa cabbage and refrigerate overnight. The next day, heat the Kimchi in a sauté pan over medium heat for 3 to 5 minutes, or until warm.

Substitutions

Pork, lamb, chicken

Wine Notes

This dish finds friendly matches in both white and red wines. Buttery California Chardonnay and plump Sangiovese do an equally good job at buffering the red-hot Kimchi and standing up to the boar. The American oak influence of vanillin spice and toast is the key. Landmark *Demeris Reserve* Chardonnay and Rabbit Ridge Sangiovese, both from California, are wines that incorporate a good dose of new wood.

All animals are equal,
    but some animals are more equal than others. — George Orwell

Pork Tenderloin with a Stir-Fry of Bitter Melon, Pig Ear Mushrooms, and Scallions Served with Wide Noodles and Spicy Curry Emulsion

Pork is ideal for serving with spicy and sharp elements, as it holds up well to strong flavors while maintaining its own identity. Here, an assertive stir-fry of bitter melon, pig ear mushrooms, and scallions is tossed together with wide, chewy noodles and topped with medallions of pork tenderloin. A spicy curry emulsion provides a sating richness. Cilantro appears three ways, in the pasta, as an oil, and scattered about in the form of sprouts. Its clean, bold flavor is the thread that weaves these exceptional elements together.

Serves 4

Cilantro Pasta (see Appendices)
1 tablespoon butter
Salt and pepper
1 tablespoon minced fresh ginger
2¹/₂ tablespoons grapeseed oil
8 scallions, tops trimmed
1¹/₂ cups pig ear mushrooms, cleaned and cut into bite-sized pieces
¹/₂ small bitter melon, thinly sliced and seeds removed
12 haricots verts
1¹/₂ cups Vegetable Stock (see Appendices)
¹/₄ cup Curry Butter (see Appendices)
8 1¹/₂-ounce pork tenderloin medallions
4 teaspoons Cilantro Oil (recipe follows)
¹/₂ cup loosely packed cilantro sprouts

METHOD To prepare the pasta: Roll out the pasta to the thinnest setting on a pasta machine. Cut the pasta into 2¹/₂-inch-wide strips. Just prior to serving, cook the noodles in boiling salted water for 2 to 3 minutes, or until al dente. Toss with the butter and season to taste with salt and pepper.

To prepare the vegetables: Sweat the ginger in 1 tablespoon of the grapeseed oil in a small sauté pan over medium-low heat for 30 seconds. Add the scallions and cook for 3 minutes. Add the mushrooms, bitter melon, and haricots verts and cook for 3 minutes, or until the vegetables are tender. Season to taste with salt and pepper.

To prepare the curry emulsion: Warm the Vegetable Stock in a small saucepan over medium heat. Whisk in the Curry Butter and season to taste with salt and pepper. Froth with a handheld blender just prior to serving.

To prepare the pork: Season the pork with salt and pepper. Place the pork in a hot sauté pan with the remaining 1¹/₂ tablespoons grapeseed oil and cook over medium-high heat for 2 to 3 minutes on each side, or until just cooked.

ASSEMBLY Arrange 2 pork medallions and some of the vegetables in the center of each plate. Drape some of the noodles over the vegetables. Spoon the curry emulsion around the plate and drizzle the Cilantro Oil around the emulsion. Sprinkle with the cilantro sprouts and top with freshly ground black pepper.

Cilantro Oil

Yield: ¹/₂ cup

¹/₂ cup firmly packed fresh cilantro leaves
1 cup firmly packed spinach
¹/₂ cup plus 1 tablespoon grapeseed oil
¹/₄ cup olive oil

Sauté the cilantro leaves and spinach with 1 tablespoon of the grapeseed oil in a small sauté pan over medium heat for 2 minutes, or until wilted. Immediately shock in ice water and drain. Coarsely chop the mixture and squeeze out the excess water. Purée the spinach mixture with the remaining ¹/₂ cup grapeseed oil and the olive oil for 3 to 4 minutes, or until bright green. Pour into a container, cover, and refrigerate for 1 day.

Strain the oil through a fine-mesh sieve and discard the solids. Refrigerate for 1 day, decant, and refrigerate until ready to use or for up to 2 weeks.

Substitutions

Chicken, lamb, poussin

Wine Notes

The strawberry fruit and herbes de Provence from the palate of a Provencal Rosé provide a not-so-obvious match for this Asian-influenced dish. Served chilled, a simple Bandol Rosé from Domaine Tempier has a pleasant cleansing effect (much like champagne), while also providing an interesting berry-fruit-flavor counterpoint for the pork, curry, and cilantro.

Duet of Terrines with Parsnip Purée, Truffle Vinaigrette, and Leek Emulsion

A terrine is a great way to begin a special meal. So, to go over the top, perhaps a duet is in order. Here, we have a beef cheek, salsify, and Belgian endive terrine and a pheasant breast, noodle, and shiitake mushroom terrine. The former is paired with a black truffle vinaigrette and the latter with a leek emulsion. A sweet, satiny purée of parsnip weaves the two elements together. Of course, either of these could be served on its own, but for the full impact I advise presenting both.

Serves 16

6 stalks salsify, peeled

2 cups milk

2 teaspoons freshly squeezed lemon juice

1 cup Pickling Juice (see Appendices)

3 heads purple Belgian endive

9 tablespoons butter

2 tablespoons sugar

Salt and pepper

12 sheets gelatin

2 cups Chicken Stock (see Appendices)

2 cups Braised Beef Cheeks (see Appendices)

2 cups Roasted Shiitake Mushrooms, (see Appendices)

2 bunches spinach, stems removed, blanched, and shocked

3 ounces perciatelli noodles, cooked al dente

2 smoked pheasant breasts, boned and skinned

1 cup peeled, chopped parsnips

1 large leek, chopped

1 cup Vegetable Stock (see Appendices)

1 black truffle, julienned

1/4 cup loosely packed micro peppercress sprouts

1/4 cup olive oil

METHOD To prepare the salsify: Place the salsify, milk, and lemon juice in a medium saucepan and cover with water. Simmer the salsify over medium-low heat for 10 to 15 minutes, or until tender. Remove the salsify from the liquid and cool. Cut 2 of the stalks into small dice. Add the diced salsify to the Pickling Juice and refrigerate for at least 1 hour. Cut the remaining salsify stalks in half lengthwise and set aside.

To prepare the endive: Quarter the endives lengthwise. Place the endive in a large sauté pan with 2 tablespoons of the butter and cook over medium-high heat for 3 to 5 minutes, or until golden brown. Add the sugar and cook for 2 minutes, or until the sugar is melted. Cool to room temperature. Season to taste with salt and pepper. Cut the root end from the endive quarters allowing the leaves to separate.

To prepare the aspic: Bloom the gelatin in a bowl of cold water for 5 minutes. Remove the gelatin from the water and place in a medium saucepan with the Chicken Stock. Cook over medium-low heat for 2 minutes, or until the gelatin is dissolved. Remove from the heat and divide the aspic between 2 bowls.

To assemble the beef cheek terrine: Line an 8 by 1½ by 2¼-inch terrine mold with plastic wrap, allowing some to drape over the sides. Dip some of the endive quarters in 1 bowl of the aspic, shaking off any excess. Lay the endive pieces in a flat layer in the bottom of the terrine mold and season with salt and pepper. Spread a ¼-inch-thick layer of the beef cheek on top of the endive, spoon some of the aspic over the beef cheek, and press firmly. Dip the halved salsify in the aspic and lay it flat on top of the beef cheek. Continue the layering process with the beef cheek, followed by the endive, beef cheek, salsify, beef cheek, and endive. Firmly press down on the terrine with your fingers or a small wooden board. Fold the excess plastic wrap over the terrine and refrigerate for 3 hours, or until set.

Preheat the oven to 400 degrees. Remove the terrine from the mold and rewrap tightly in plastic wrap. With the plastic wrap on, cut the terrine into 16 slices. Lay the slices on a parchment-lined sheet tray and carefully remove the plastic wrap. Season to taste with salt and pepper. Just prior to serving, flash the terrine in the oven for 1 to 2 minutes to remove the chill.

To assemble the pheasant terrine: Line an 8 by 1½ by 2¼-inch terrine mold with plastic wrap, allowing some to drape over the sides. Dip the shiitake mushrooms in the second bowl of aspic, shaking off any excess. Lay the mushrooms in a flat layer in the bottom of the terrine mold. Season with salt and pepper. Arrange some of the spinach over the mushrooms and spoon some of the aspic over the spinach. Again, season with salt and pepper. Arrange some of the noodles over the spinach and spoon some of the aspic over the noodles, seasoning again. Arrange a layer of spinach, mushrooms, and then another layer of spinach in the terrine, seasoning with salt and pepper after each layer. Cut the pheasant breasts to fit the width of the terrine and form a layer, using the trimmings to fill in the holes. Complete the layering process with spinach, mushrooms, spinach, noodles, spinach, and ending with a layer of

continued on page 233

Black Olive-and-Mushroom–Stuffed Pork Belly with Caper Berries and Garlic Chives

Pork belly is rich and succulent, which is why it works perfectly with notes of olive, anchovy, and caper that cut into the fat. In this case, those ingredients are suspended in wild mushrooms that serve as the stuffing. Garlic chives and caper berries add additional balance, and a drizzle of meat reduction provides a note of richness to round things out.

Serves 4

3 cups wild mushrooms (such as chanterelles, oyster, or porcini), cleaned

2 tablespoons minced shallot

2 tablespoons butter

½ cup chopped kalamata olives

½ cup capers, rinsed

1 tablespoon chopped fresh flat-leaf parsley

¾ cup ground pork

¼ cup ground pork fat

15 salt-packed anchovies, filleted, rinsed, and chopped

Salt and pepper

1 1½-pound baby pork belly

3 tablespoons grapeseed oil

28 fresh garlic chives

1 tablespoon olive oil

8 caper berries, thinly sliced

½ cup Meat Stock Reduction (see Appendices)

METHOD To prepare the pork belly: Preheat the oven to 400 degrees. Cook the mushrooms, shallot, and butter in a hot sauté pan over medium heat for 5 minutes, or until the mushrooms are tender. Finely chop the mushrooms and place in a large bowl with the olives, capers, parsley, ground pork and pork fat, and anchovies. Toss the ingredients together and season to taste with salt and pepper.

Place the pork belly on a cutting board and insert a long, very sharp knife through the side of the cut end of the belly, creating a pocket that goes through to the other side. Using a pastry bag fitted with a ½-inch tip, fill the pork belly with the mushroom mixture. Place the pork belly in a hot sauté pan with the grapeseed oil and cook over medium heat for 5 minutes on each side, or until golden brown. Roast the pork belly in the oven for 40 to 50 minutes, or until cooked. Remove from the oven and let rest for 5 minutes. Cut into 1-inch-thick pieces.

To prepare the garlic chives and caper berries: Cook the garlic chives in the olive oil in a small sauté pan over medium heat for 2 minutes, or until hot.

Place the caper berries in a saucepan with the Meat Stock Reduction and warm over medium heat for 3 minutes, or until hot.

ASSEMBLY Arrange some of the wilted garlic chives and a slice of the pork belly at an angle in the center of each plate. Spoon the caper berries and Meat Stock Reduction around the plate and top with freshly ground black pepper.

Substitutions

Slab bacon, pork

Wine Notes

The capers and kalamata olives give this dish a Mediterranean feel. A warm-climate red from the south of France, Mas de Gourgonnier, from the appellation Les Baux de Provence, is a fun possibility. Comprised of Grenache, Mourvèdre, Syrah, and others, it is a deep, spice-charged red that is a match for the chewy pork belly, piquant capers, and spicy garlic chives.

Lamb Rack with Cumin-Scented Porcini Mushrooms, Golden Raisins, and Potato Purée

~~~~~~~~~~~~~~~~~~~~~~~~~~~~~~~~~~~~~

This dish features the succulent texture and delicately assertive flavor of lamb against extravagant cumin-scented porcini mushroom pieces. The controlled sweetness of the plumped raisins not only cuts into the luscious fat on the lamb, but also nicely accentuates the profound flavor of the cumin. A loose purée of potato adds substance and a sensual mouthfeel. Oregano leaves deliver the perfect whimsical accent.

Serves 4

2 cups sliced porcini mushrooms

1½ tablespoons butter

1 tablespoon coarsely ground cumin seeds

1 tablespoon rice vinegar

⅓ cup water

1 tablespoon olive oil

½ cup golden raisins

Salt and pepper

1 large lamb rack with 4 chops, frenched

1½ tablespoons grapeseed oil

1½ cups Potato Purée (see Appendices)

8 teaspoons Oregano Oil (recipe follows)

4 teaspoons small fresh oregano leaves

METHOD To prepare the mushrooms: Place the mushrooms in a sauté pan with the butter and 1 teaspoon of the cumin and sauté over medium heat for 2 minutes. Add the rice vinegar, water, olive oil, and golden raisins and cook for 3 minutes, or until the mushrooms are tender. Season to taste with salt and pepper.

To prepare the lamb: Preheat the oven to 400 degrees. Season the lamb with salt and pepper and sprinkle with the remaining 2 teaspoons cumin. Place the lamb in a hot roasting pan with the grapeseed oil and sear over medium-high heat for 3 minutes on each side. Roast in the oven for 15 minutes, or until cooked medium-rare. Let rest for 3 minutes and slice the rack into 4 chops.

ASSEMBLY Spoon a large ring of the warm Potato Purée onto each plate. Spoon the mushroom mixture along with any juices that remain in the pan into the center of the ring. Place a lamb chop over the mushrooms and drizzle the Oregano Oil around the plate. Sprinkle with the oregano leaves and top with freshly ground black pepper.

Oregano Oil

Yield: ½ cup

½ cup firmly packed fresh oregano leaves

1 cup firmly packed spinach

½ cup plus 1 tablespoon grapeseed oil

¼ cup olive oil

METHOD Sauté the oregano leaves and spinach with 1 tablespoon of the grapeseed oil in a small sauté pan over medium heat for 2 minutes, or until wilted. Immediately shock in ice water and drain. Coarsely chop the mixture and squeeze out the excess water. Purée the spinach mixture with the remaining ½ cup grapeseed oil and the olive oil for 3 to 4 minutes, or until bright green. Pour into a container, cover, and refrigerate for 1 day.

Strain the oil through a fine-mesh sieve and discard the solids. Refrigerate for 1 day, decant, and refrigerate until ready to use or for up to 2 weeks.

Substitutions

Beef, pork, chicken, veal

Wine Notes

While the spicy cumin and fragrant oregano ask for Cabernet Franc, the sweet raisins demand a New World style. Nelson Estate in Sonoma produces a spicy style that handles the strong herbaceous notes with big, extracted fruit.

Everything in a pig is good.
What ingratitude has permitted his name to become a term of opprobrium

RIMOD DE LAS REYNIÈRE

Deconstructed Cassoulet

This preparation takes a few liberties with a classic dish, but it is designed to show off the elements in a more singular fashion, rather than having their flavors and textures meld into one. The addition of white truffle slices at the last moment elevates the dish. A small salad served on the side would nicely set off the luscious creation.

Serves 8

1 cup julienned bacon

¼ cup minced shallot

2 cups dried rice beans, soaked in water overnight

6 cloves garlic

2 cups tomato concassé

3 cups Chicken Stock (see Appendices)

2 sprigs rosemary

Salt and pepper

¼ cup chopped fresh flat-leaf parsley

1 pound Braised Black Pig Shoulder, hot (see Appendices)

½ cup Meat Stock Reduction, hot (see Appendices)

1 small white truffle, thinly shaved

4 teaspoons tiny fresh flat-leaf parsley leaves

METHOD To prepare the rice beans: Cook the bacon in a large saucepan over medium heat for 4 minutes, or until the fat is rendered. Add the shallot and cook for 3 minutes, or until translucent. Drain the rice beans and add them to the saucepan along with the garlic cloves, tomato concassé, and Chicken Stock. Slowly simmer the beans over medium-low heat for 3 to 4 hours, or until extremely tender. (Additional stock or water may be added if necessary.) Add the rosemary and season to taste with salt and pepper. Simmer for 15 minutes and remove the rosemary. Fold in the chopped parsley and keep warm.

ASSEMBLY Slice the braised pig into 16 thick slices and season to taste with salt and pepper. Spoon some of the braised beans in a diagonal line in the center of each plate. Place 2 slices of the braised black pig over the beans. Spoon the Meat Stock Reduction over the meat and sprinkle with the white truffle and parsley leaves. Top with freshly ground black pepper.

Substitutions

Suckling pig, veal, pork

Wine Notes

The hearty components of this dish, perfect for a warm winter night, are best matched with a reassuringly full-bodied red. The tannins in powerful left bank Bordeaux are tamed by the well-marbled pork and bacon. Rich, dense Cabernet Sauvignon–based wines from the commune of Pauillac, such as the noble Château Lafite-Rothschild or its cousin, Duhart-Milon, will keep everyone warm.

Bison Bone Marrow Flan
with Porcini Mushroom Crust and Sage

This preparation is indeed an incredible treat. The flan cooked inside the bone is decadently rich—
fortunately, it's a small portion. Earthy porcini mushrooms, both sautéed and puréed,
further accentuate the delicate flavor of the flan. A little meat juice and some sage or thyme are
all that is needed to round out the dish. This makes a great first course for a special meal.

Serves 4

8 2-inch pieces bison bones

3 eggs

1 cup heavy whipping cream

Salt and pepper

¼ cup butter

*½ cup Veal Stock Reduction
(see Appendices)*

Grapeseed oil for deep-frying

20 ⅛-inch-thick slices porcini mushrooms

1 cup brunoise-cut porcini mushrooms

1 tablespoon chopped flat-leaf parsley

½ cup chopped fresh porcini mushrooms

1 teaspoon minced shallot

¼ cup water

4 teaspoons tiny fresh sage leaves

METHOD To prepare the flan: Preheat the oven to 325 degrees. Place the bones in boiling salted water for 10 minutes, or until the marrow is tender. Remove from the water and cool to room temperature. Push the marrow out of the bones, reserving the marrow and the bones separately. Reserve the 4 nicest bones with flat bottoms and discard the remainder. Purée the marrow from 4 of the bones with the eggs until smooth. Whisk the cream into the egg mixture and season with salt and pepper.

Wrap the bottom of the bones tightly with plastic wrap and aluminum foil. Stand the bones upright in an ovenproof pan with 2-inch sides. Pour the flan into the bones and add water to a depth of 1 inch to the pan. Bake for 30 to 40 minutes, or until just set. Remove the flans from the water bath and release the plastic wrap just prior to serving.

Slice the remaining marrow into ½-inch-thick slices and place in a sauté pan with 1 tablespoon of the butter. Cook over medium heat for 1 minute on each side. Add 5 tablespoons of the Veal Stock Reduction and cook for 1 minute, or until hot.

To prepare the fried porcini: Pour grapeseed oil to a depth of 1 inch into a medium sauté pan. Add the sliced mushrooms, place over medium heat, and cook for 5 to 7 minutes, or until golden brown and crispy. Remove from the oil, blot on paper towels, and season to taste with salt.

To prepare the porcini crust: Place 2 tablespoons of the butter in a small sauté pan and cook over medium-low heat until it is brown and has a nutty aroma. Add the brunoise-cut mushrooms and cook for 3 minutes over medium heat, or until the mushrooms are tender. Add the remaining 3 tablespoons Veal Stock Reduction and cook for 2 minutes. Season to taste with salt and pepper and fold in the parsley.

To prepare the porcini purée: Sauté the chopped porcini mushrooms and shallot with the remaining 1 tablespoon butter in a sauté pan over medium heat for 4 minutes, or until tender. Purée with the water until smooth. Season to taste with salt and pepper and warm in a small saucepan just prior to serving.

ASSEMBLY Place 1 bone marrow flan in the center of each plate. Place a mound of the brunoise porcini mushrooms over the flan. Arrange some of the bone marrow slices, fried mushrooms, and mushroom purée around the flan. Sprinkle the sage leaves around the plate and top with freshly ground black pepper.

Substitutions

Beef marrow, wild mushroom custard

Wine Notes

A mature, seductive Barolo from Italy is a classic match for this modern interpretation of osso buco. The earthy Nebbiolo-based reds are a decadent pairing for the buttery flan and the porcini mushrooms three ways. The wines from the village of La Morra are regarded as the most supple and forward of the Barolos. Ceretto's single vineyard reds *Brunate* and *Bricco Roche* should not be missed.

Robust Meat
& Game

Veal Tenderloin, Maine Lobster, Asparagus, and Squash Blossoms with Verjus-Lobster Broth and Chervil

This preparation has achieved an almost stewlike consistency by the time you serve it.
Although everything is cooked separately, the flavors and textures meld together perfectly.
The rich lobster broth is cut by the complex flavor of the verjus and the tomatoes that have
been cooked in it. Chervil provides just the right floral note, helping to keep things fresh and light.
If a more substantial dish were desired, mushrooms or pasta could easily be added.

Serves 4

8 shallots, thinly sliced

¼ cup butter

1 cup red wine verjus

3 cups Shellfish Stock (see Appendices)

1 cup red teardrop tomatoes, halved

1 cup yellow teardrop tomatoes, halved

12 green asparagus spears, parboiled and halved on the diagonal

8 squash blossoms, halved lengthwise and pistils removed

2 small Maine lobster tails, cooked, shelled, and each cut into 6 slices

Salt and pepper

2 ounces tiny white asparagus

1 cup milk

1 12-ounce veal tenderloin

2 teaspoons grapeseed oil

1 teaspoon fleur de sel

4 teaspoons chopped fresh chervil

4 teaspoons Chervil Oil (recipe follows)

METHOD To prepare the broth: Cook the shallots and butter in a saucepan over medium heat for 3 to 4 minutes, or until translucent. Deglaze with the red wine verjus. Add the Shellfish Stock and tomatoes and simmer for 3 minutes. Just before serving, add the green asparagus, squash blossoms, and lobster. Cook for 1 minute and season to taste with salt and pepper.

To prepare the white asparagus: Warm the white asparagus in the milk in a small saucepan over medium-low heat for 2 minutes, or until tender. Remove from the milk and rinse. Season with salt and pepper.

To prepare the veal: Season the veal with salt and pepper. Place in a hot sauté pan with the grapeseed oil and cook over medium-high heat for 3 minutes on each side, or until cooked medium-rare. Let rest for 3 minutes. Cut the tenderloin into 16 equal slices and season to taste with salt and pepper.

ASSEMBLY Ladle some of the broth into each bowl, being careful to get some of each ingredient. Place 4 slices of the veal in the center of the bowl, and top with some of the white asparagus. Sprinkle the fleur de sel and chopped chervil over the veal and drizzle the Chervil Oil around the bowl.

Chervil Oil

Yield: ½ cup

½ cup firmly packed fresh chervil leaves
1 cup firmly packed spinach
½ cup plus 1 tablespoon grapeseed oil
¼ cup olive oil

METHOD Sauté the chervil leaves and spinach with 1 tablespoon of the grapeseed oil in a small sauté pan over medium heat for 2 minutes, or until wilted. Immediately shock in ice water and drain. Coarsely chop the mixture and squeeze out the excess water. Purée the spinach mixture with the remaining ½ cup grapeseed oil and the olive oil for 3 to 4 minutes, or until bright green. Pour into a container, cover, and refrigerate for 1 day.

Strain the oil through a fine-mesh sieve and discard the solids. Refrigerate for 1 day, decant, and refrigerate until ready to use or for up to 2 weeks.

Substitutions

Beef, pork, crayfish, shrimp

Wine Notes

The elegant broth is in very delicate balance with the rich veal, buttery lobster, and vegetable elements. Oak is the enemy of this dish. One pairing possibility is Riesling Spätlese Trocken, such as Hocheimer Steilweg from Franz Kunstler. It displays clean, pure fruit and a dry, racy finish that refreshes. Or, try Jermann's *Vintage Tunina* from Friuli-Venezia in Italy, a blend of aromatic white wine grapes (including Sauvignon Blanc) that has a zesty acidity for the asparagus and tomatoes and enough body to support the dish.

Braised Black Pig Shoulder with Wild Mushroom Package, Kaffir Lime–Curry Emulsion, and Lentil Purée

*By slowly braising the shoulder of the black pig an incredibly succulent result can be achieved.
Here the meat is paired with an earthy package of wild mushrooms. A lentil purée
adds a further rustic note, but the whole composition takes on a stunning transcendence with the
assertive but ultra-light kaffir lime–curry emulsion. This preparation could work
as a light appetizer, or its portion size could be increased and it would work fabulously as an entrée.*

Serves 4

*1 cup French green lentils,
soaked in water for 4 hours*

2 ounces slab bacon, cut into large chunks

1/2 cup large-diced carrot

1/2 cup large-diced celery

1 cup large-diced Spanish onion

4 cups Chicken Stock (see Appendices)

Salt and pepper

3 cups hen of the woods mushrooms, cleaned

1 shallot, minced

1 1/2 tablespoons butter

4 heads baby kohlrabi, quartered

1 2-inch piece daikon

3 cups Vegetable Stock (see Appendices)

*4 large Swiss chard leaves, blanched and
shocked and stems removed*

4 kaffir lime leaves, crushed

1/4 cup Curry Butter (see Appendices)

2 heads baby bok choy, steamed and halved

*Braised Black Pig Shoulder, braising liquid
reserved (see Appendices)*

2 tablespoons micro radish sprouts

METHOD To prepare the lentils: Drain the lentils and set aside. Cook the bacon in a large saucepan over medium heat for 5 minutes, or until the fat is rendered. Add the carrot, celery, and onion and cook for 3 to 5 minutes, or until the vegetables are caramelized. Add the lentils and Chicken Stock and simmer over medium-low heat for 1 hour, or until the lentils are tender.Remove the vegetables and bacon and discard. Season the lentils to taste with salt and pepper.

Remove half of the lentils from the pan with a slotted spoon and set aside. Purée the remaining lentils and any cooking juices that remain in the pan until smooth. Season to taste with salt and pepper.

To prepare the mushroom packages: Preheat the oven to 350 degrees. Cook the mushrooms and shallot with the butter in a medium sauté pan over medium heat for 5 to 7 minutes, or until tender. Season to taste with salt and pepper, chop coarsely, and set aside.

Place the kohlrabis and daikon in a small saucepan with the Vegetable Stock and simmer over medium heat for 10 minutes, or until tender. Remove the kohlrabis and daikon and reserve the cooking liquid for the emulsion. Reserve 8 pieces of the kohlrabi and coarsely chop the remaining kohlrabi. Season to taste with salt and pepper. Slice the daikon into thin disks and season to taste with salt and pepper.

Place the chopped mushrooms and kohlrabi in a small bowl and toss together. Lay the Swiss chard leaves flat and remove the thick inner spine from each leaf, leaving the leaf in one piece. Season the inner side of the chard with salt and pepper. Spoon one-fourth of the mushroom mixture into the middle of each Swiss chard leaf and carefully roll up, folding the sides in, to create a shape similar to a thick cigar. Just prior to serving, bake for 3 to 5 minutes, or until just warm. Trim the ends and cut each package into 2 pieces.

To prepare the emulsion: Reheat the reserved cooking liquid from the kohlrabi with the kaffir lime leaves in a small saucepan for 5 minutes, or until hot. Whisk in the Curry Butter and season to taste with salt and pepper. Froth with a handheld mixer just prior to serving.

ASSEMBLY Stand a piece of the mushroom package up at the top of each plate. Arrange the daikon, bok choy, and kohlrabi in front of the mushroom package. Lean a piece of the braised black pig over the vegetables. Spoon the lentil purée and lentils around the plate. Spoon the kaffir lime–curry emulsion over the mushroom package and around the plate. Spoon some of the reduced braising liquid over the black pig, and sprinkle the radish sprouts around the plate.

Substitutions

Lamb shoulder, pork leg, veal breast

Wine Notes

The lime-scented curry emulsion, braised lentils, and wild mushrooms find a lively match in St. Joseph Blanc. One-hundred-percent Marsanne, grown in the northern Rhône Valley, goes into Yves Cuilleron's St. Joseph *Cuvée Izeras*. It is a vibrant, zesty, dry white that works with the vegetables and has the body to support the ginger-scented pork.

Antelope Loin with Yellow and Red Plums and Porcini Mushrooms

This combination is simple enough, but the flavors come together in a most profound way.
The antelope loin is full flavored but not too assertive, and it is balanced perfectly by the sweet
acidity of the plums and the elegant earthiness of the porcini mushrooms. Plum juices
and red wine make up the sauce, and a little rosemary is all that is needed to finish the plate.

Serves 4

6 small porcini mushrooms, cleaned

1/2 cup plus 2 tablespoons water

1 sprig thyme

Salt and pepper

1 teaspoon minced shallot

3 tablespoons butter

2 red plums, skin on, halved and pitted

2 teaspoons sugar

1 sprig rosemary

1/2 cup plus 3 tablespoons red wine

1 red plum, peeled, pitted, and chopped

*1/2 cup Venison Stock Reduction
(see Appendices)*

1 1-pound antelope tenderloin

2 teaspoons grapeseed oil

*1 yellow plum, peeled, pitted, and
medium diced*

2 teaspoons fresh rosemary leaves

METHOD To prepare the mushrooms: Preheat the oven to 350 degrees. Place the mushrooms, 1/2 cup of the water, and the thyme sprig in an ovenproof pan and season with salt and pepper. Cover with aluminum foil and roast for 30 minutes, or until tender. Just prior to serving, slice the mushrooms in half and sauté with the shallot and 1 tablespoon of the butter over medium heat for 3 minutes, or until hot. Season to taste with salt and pepper.

To prepare the roasted plums: Place the red plum halves, skin side up, in an ovenproof pan with 1 tablespoon of the butter, the sugar, the rosemary, and 3 tablespoons of the red wine. Cover with aluminum foil and roast for 30 minutes, or until the skin is easily removed from the plums. Discard the plum skin. Cut the plum halves into quarters and toss with the juices from the pan.

To prepare the sauce: Place the chopped red plum and the remaining 1/2 cup red wine, the Venison Stock Reduction, and the remaining 2 tablespoons water in a small saucepan. Cook the plums over low heat for 20 minutes. Pass the mixture through a fine-mesh sieve and season to taste with salt and pepper.

To prepare the antelope: Season the antelope tenderloin with salt and pepper. Place the tenderloin in a hot sauté pan with the grapeseed oil and cook over medium-high heat for 4 minutes on each side, or until cooked medium-rare. Let rest for 3 minutes. Cut into 12 equal slices and season to taste with salt and pepper.

To prepare the diced plum: Place the diced yellow plum in a hot sauté pan with the remaining 1 tablespoon butter and 1 teaspoon of the rosemary leaves and cook over medium heat for 3 minutes, or until tender.

ASSEMBLY Arrange some of the mushrooms and red plum pieces on the plate. Arrange 3 slices of the antelope in the center of the plate and spoon the diced yellow plums around the plate. Spoon the red wine–plum sauce around the plate and sprinkle with the remaining 1 teaspoon rosemary leaves.

Substitutions

Venison, beef, lamb

Wine Notes

The sweet plums made savory by the fragrant rosemary are a graceful accompaniment to the antelope and porcini mushrooms. There is a delicate equilibrium to this course that would be destroyed by a heavy-handed red wine match. Choose instead a fruity white with density. An interesting treat is Nuits-St.-Georges *Les Perrières* Blanc from Domaine Henri Gouges. Vinified from their own unusual *Albino* Pinot Noir grapes, it is a lighter-style red that masquerades as a white.

Lamb Loin with Acidic Parsnips
and Green Curry Sauce

*In this preparation, the lamb loin shows off wonderfully against the
refined spiciness of the Green Curry Sauce and the clean acidity of the parsnip pieces.
Small, round carrots provide just the right sweet element to offset the parsnip.
Lightly wilted spinach leaves and a few micro sprouts punctuate the dish nicely.
The final result is a combination that seems boldly flavored but is actually quite elegant.*

Serves 4

1 large parsnip, peeled

1 cup Pickling Juice (see Appendices)

1/2 teaspoon fresh thyme leaves

1/2 teaspoon fresh rosemary leaves

1/2 teaspoon fenugreek seeds

4 round carrots, parboiled

1 teaspoon butter

1 cup firmly packed baby spinach

Salt and pepper

1 8-ounce lamb tenderloin

1 teaspoon grapeseed oil

Green Curry Sauce (recipe follows)

*1/4 cup Lamb Stock Reduction, hot
(see Appendices)*

1 1/2 tablespoons micro arugula sprouts

METHOD To prepare the parsnip: Cut the parsnip into long, wide strips using a vegetable peeler. Place the parsnip strips in a small saucepan with the Pickling Juice and cook over medium heat for 5 minutes, or until tender. Remove from the Pickling Juice just prior to serving.

To prepare the carrots: Place the thyme, rosemary, and fenugreek in a small bowl and toss together. Cut the carrots in half lengthwise, place in a sauté pan with the butter, and cook over medium heat for 3 minutes, or until caramelized. Add half of the spice mixture, cook for 1 minute, and remove the carrots from the pan. Add the spinach to the pan and cook over medium heat for 2 minutes, or until wilted. Season to taste with salt and pepper.

To prepare the lamb: Season the lamb with salt and pepper. Place in a hot sauté pan with the grapeseed oil and cook over medium-high heat for 3 minutes on each side, or until cooked medium-rare. Let rest for 3 minutes. Cut into 20 equal slices and season to taste with salt and pepper.

ASSEMBLY Arrange the parsnip strips and spinach in the center of each plate. Arrange 5 lamb slices and 2 carrot halves around the plate. Spoon on the Green Curry Sauce and Lamb Stock Reduction, and sprinkle with the arugula sprouts and remaining spice mixture.

Green Curry Sauce

Yield: approximately 2 cups

1 large Spanish onion, sliced

1 tablespoon minced fresh ginger

1 1/2 tablespoons minced garlic

3 green Thai chiles

1/2 cup grapeseed oil

2 tomatoes, chopped

1 tablespoon ajowan seeds

6 cardamom pods, shells removed

1/2 cinnamon stick

2 bay leaves

1 tablespoon ground turmeric

1 tablespoon coriander seeds, crushed

1 cup Vegetable Stock (see Appendices)

*2 cups firmly packed cilantro leaves,
blanched and shocked*

*2 cups firmly packed mint leaves,
blanched and shocked*

*4 cups firmly packed spinach,
blanched and shocked*

1 cup plain yogurt

Salt and pepper

METHOD Sauté the onion, ginger, garlic, and Thai chiles in 1 tablespoon of the grapeseed oil in a medium sauté pan over medium heat for 5 minutes, or until the garlic has a nutty aroma. Add the tomatoes, ajowan seeds, cardamom, cinnamon, bay leaves, turmeric, and coriander and cook for 5 minutes, or until very aromatic. Add the Vegetable Stock, bring to a boil, and purée until smooth. Strain through a fine-mesh sieve. Purée the cilantro, mint, and spinach with the remaining 7 tablespoons grapeseed oil until smooth.

Combine the Vegetable Stock purée, herb purée, and yogurt in a medium saucepan over medium heat and cook for 10 minutes, or until warm. Season with salt and pepper.

Substitutions

Beef, squab, chicken

Wine Notes

The lamb loin has a strong presence, elevating the dish to a red wine–friendly presentation. The pickled parsnip and frgrant green curry mandate that the wine have a bright profile like the Pinot Noirs from the Côte Chalonnaise. From the village of Mercurey, Faiveley's *Clos des Myglands* displays characteristic red berry fruit and firm acidity. The tangy, high-toned red serves the spectrum of flavors well.

KODAK EPT 6037   50

Venison with Saffron Cabbage
and Beef Tongue Sauce

*This preparation nicely contrasts the playful assertive pepper on the robust venison meat with
the soothing character of the saffron-flavored napa cabbage. A sauce made by dicing
slowly braised beef tongue and using some of the braising liquid is spooned about the meat.
The result is an absolutely soul-satisfying composition of sensual flavors.*

Serves 4

1 beef tongue

Salt and pepper

3 tablespoons grapeseed oil

3 large carrots, cut into ³/₄-inch-thick slices

1¹/₂ cups chopped Spanish onion

2 leeks, chopped

2 quarts Beef Stock (see Appendices)

1 teaspoon black peppercorns

1 bulb garlic, halved

8 sprigs thyme

2 bay leaves

1 cup sherry

2 sprigs rosemary

*1¹/₂ tablespoons chopped fresh
flat-leaf parsley*

Pinch of saffron threads

5 tablespoons butter

8 leaves napa cabbage, cut into 2-inch pieces

1 cup hon-shimeji mushrooms, cleaned

1 tablespoon minced shallot

1 teaspoon sherry wine vinegar

*4 3-ounce venison medallions,
tied with butcher's twine*

2 teaspoons pink peppercorns, crushed

2 teaspoons green peppercorns, crushed

1 teaspoon fleur de sel

METHOD To prepare the beef tongue: Preheat the oven to 250 degrees. Season the beef tongue with salt and pepper. Sear the tongue with 2 tablespoons of the grapeseed oil in a hot braising pan over medium-high heat for 3 minutes on each side, or until golden brown. Remove the tongue from the pan and add the carrots, onion, and leeks. Cook for 5 to 7 minutes, or until golden brown. Return the tongue to the pan and add the stock, black peppercorns, garlic, thyme, bay leaves, sherry, and rosemary. Bring the mixture to a simmer, cover, and place in the oven. Braise the tongue for 4 to 5 hours, or until tender. Remove the tongue from the liquid, cool, and peel off the skin. Cut the tongue into ¹/₂-inch dice and season to taste with salt and pepper.

Strain the braising liquid and pick out the carrots, discarding the other vegetables. Cut the carrots into ¹/₂-inch dice, discarding the trimmings. Place the braising liquid in a saucepan and simmer over medium heat for 30 to 40 minutes, or until reduced to ¹/₂ cup. Add the parsley and season to taste with pepper. Warm just prior to serving.

To prepare the cabbage: Place the saffron in a sauté pan over medium heat for 30 seconds, or until aromatic. Add 3 tablespoons of the butter and the cabbage and cook for 6 to 8 minutes, or until the cabbage is wilted. Season to taste with salt and pepper.

To prepare the mushrooms: Sauté the mushrooms and shallot with the remaining 2 tablespoons butter in a small sauté pan over medium-high heat for 3 to 4 minutes, or until the mushrooms are tender. Add the sherry wine vinegar and season to taste with salt and pepper.

To prepare the venison: Season the venison with salt and sprinkle with the pink and green peppercorns. Place the venison in a hot sauté pan with the remaining 1 tablespoon grapeseed oil and cook over medium-high heat for 3 minutes on each side, or until medium-rare. Remove from the pan and let rest for 2 minutes. Slice the medallions in half horizontally.

ASSEMBLY Place some of the cabbage and mushrooms in the center of each plate. Spoon any excess cooking liquid over and around the cabbage and place 2 slices of the venison over the cabbage. Arrange the diced carrots and beef tongue around the plate. Spoon some of the beef tongue reduction over and around the tongue and carrots. Sprinkle the fleur de sel on the tongue.

Substitutions

Lamb, beef, veal

Wine Notes

With peppery venison, caramelized sweetness from the beef tongue sauce, and the rustic vegetal character of the cabbage ennobled by saffron, a multifaceted red is needed. The southern Rhône Valley's blended Châteauneuf-du-Pape works well with the many flavors here. Choose a producer who leans toward a fuller-bodied style such as Château Fortia, whose blend boasts a higher percentage of Syrah.

Loin of Scottish Hare with Braised Sprouted Legumes, Cauliflower, Barbaresco Emulsion, and Juniper-Scented Hare Jus

This preparation is full flavored, but all of the elements have their place and shine through. Nonetheless, the loin of hare is the star. The earthy components—the legumes, cauliflower, and collard greens—provide just the right backdrop for the succulent, bold-flavored meat. Hare jus, infused with juniper, helps to bring the flavors together with a poignant note from the spice. An emulsion of reduced Barbaresco provides acid and a luscious sultriness. A twist of pepper and some summer savory leaves add the final provocative accents of flavor.

Serves 4

1 cup fresh sprouted legumes

3 tablespoons butter

1 sprig summer savory

Salt and pepper

¼ cup bacon batons

4 cups loosely packed chopped collard greens

3 tablespoons balsamic vinegar

1½ tablespoons brown sugar

2 cups water

½ head cauliflower

2 tablespoons grapeseed oil

3 Scottish hare tenderloins (about 9 ounces)

½ cup Hare Stock Reduction (see Appendices)

3 juniper berries

1 cup Barbaresco Emulsion (recipe follows)

4 teaspoons fresh summer savory leaves

METHOD To prepare the legumes: Place the legumes in a saucepan with the butter and savory sprig. Cover with 1 inch of water and simmer over low heat for 30 to 50 minutes, or until the legumes are very tender. Drain well and season with salt and pepper.

To prepare the collard greens: Cook the bacon in a sauté pan over medium heat for 7 to 8 minutes, or until the fat is rendered. Add the collard greens and coat with the bacon fat. Add the balsamic vinegar, brown sugar, and water. Cover and cook over low heat for 30 to 40 minutes, or until the greens are very tender. Season with salt and pepper.

To prepare the cauliflower: Cut two ¼-inch-thick slices from the cauliflower. Remove the excess core and trim each slice into 6 uniform pieces. Season with salt and pepper. Place the cauliflower pieces in a hot sauté pan with 1 tablespoon of the grapeseed oil and cook over medium-high heat for 2 to 3 minutes on each side, or until golden brown.

To prepare the hare: Season the hare with salt and pepper. Place in a hot sauté pan with 1 tablespoon grapeseed oil and cook over medium-high heat for 2 minutes on each side, or until cooked medium. Let rest for 5 minutes. Trim the edges of each tenderloin straight and cut into 4 equal medallions. Season with salt and pepper.

To prepare the hare jus: Bring the Hare Stock Reduction to a simmer in a small saucepan. Add the juniper berries and cook for 3 minutes. Remove from the heat. Remove the berries with a slotted spoon and discard.

ASSEMBLY Spoon some of the collard greens in the center of each plate and top with 3 pieces of cauliflower. Place the legumes at 4 points around the plate. Place a piece of hare on top of each piece of cauliflower, and spoon the hare jus and Barbaresco Emulsion around the plate. Sprinkle with the summer savory leaves and top with freshly ground black pepper.

Barbaresco Emulsion

Yield: 1 cup

1½ cups chopped Spanish onion

1 cup chopped carrot

1 cup chopped celery

2 tablespoons grapeseed oil

1 Granny Smith apple, peeled and chopped

1 orange, peeled, chopped

6 cups Barbaresco

3 cups Port

3 tablespoons butter

METHOD Cook the onion, carrot, and celery in the grapeseed oil in a large saucepan over high heat for 10 minutes, or until golden brown and caramelized. Add the apple, orange, wine, and Port and simmer over medium heat for 1 hour.

Strain through a fine-mesh sieve and return the liquid to the saucepan. Simmer for 30 to 45 minutes, or until reduced to 1 cup. Just prior to using, whisk in the butter and froth with a handheld blender.

Substitutions

Rabbit, beef, veal

Wine Notes

The sweet, smoky, bacon-infused collard greens, dark hare meat, and Barbaresco Emulsion make red wine the indisputable choice here. The juniper-scented hare jus and sweet greens are well met by Tuscan Sangiovese that has been enhanced by new oak aging. *Il Carbanione* from Podere Poggio Scalette adds a dimension of ripe, deep fruit, while punctuating the meatiness of the hare.

Matsuzaka Beef with Burmese Red Rice, Porcini Mushrooms, and Mushroom Purée

This beef, one of the truly great luxury items, is so fat and unctuous that it just melts in your mouth. Here, it is paired with chewy and aromatic Burmese red rice and pieces of heady porcini mushrooms. Indeed, the mushrooms are probably "meatier" than the beef. The wonderful thing about this preparation, however, is that each of the three elements holds its own against the others. A drizzle of meat juice and porcini purée soothingly rounds out the plate.

Serves 4

3 cups porcini mushrooms, cleaned

2 tablespoons olive oil

Salt and pepper

1/2 cup Chicken Stock (see Appendices)

1 12-ounce Matsuzaka beef strip loin

1/2 cup sea salt

1 cup sake

1 cup tamari soy sauce

1 1/2 cups cooked Burmese red rice

1/2 cup Meat Stock Reduction, hot (see Appendices)

2 teaspoons fresh rosemary leaves

METHOD To prepare the mushrooms: Slice the mushrooms 1/4 inch thick, keeping the caps attached if possible. Lightly brush the slices with the olive oil and season with salt and pepper. Grill over medium heat for 2 minutes on each side, or until cooked. Purée one-third of the mushrooms with just enough of the stock to make a smooth sauce. Season to taste with salt and pepper and warm in a saucepan over medium heat just prior to serving.

To prepare the beef: Crust the beef in the sea salt and grill over very high heat for 2 minutes on each side. Remove the meat from the grill and rinse with the sake. Return to the hot grill and cook for 30 seconds on each side. Remove the meat a second time and rinse in the tamari. Return the meat to the grill, lower the heat to medium, and cook for 2 to 3 minutes on each side, or until cooked medium-rare. Let rest for 3 minutes. Cut into 1/4-inch-thick slices and season with salt and pepper.

ASSEMBLY Spoon some of the rice in the center of each plate. Arrange the sliced mushrooms over the rice and place 3 slices of the meat over the mushrooms. Spoon the mushroom purée and Meat Stock Reduction around the plate and sprinkle with the rosemary leaves.

Substitutions

Beef strip loin, veal, lamb

Wine Notes

The strong flavors of the melt-in-your-mouth Matsuzaka beef and Burmese red rice make south Australian Mourvèdre an interesting proposition. In the Barossa Valley, Dan Hewittson produces a distinctive style that smells of leather and barnyards. It has the perfect texture for the densely marbled red meat and matches up nicely with the earthy rice and porcini mushrooms.

Braised Beef Short Ribs with Horseradish-Potato Purée, Parslied Shallots, and Red Wine Jus

Food doesn't get any more soulful than this. The short ribs are cooked to the point at which a spoon is all that is needed to shred the meat. The horseradish-potato purée provides a creamy, satiny element, with a playful bite. Roasted parslied shallots and Red Wine Jus help to lighten the richness of the meat, and grated horseradish adds a final note of lively heat that splendidly finishes the dish.

Serves 4

8 short ribs, trimmed of excess fat

Salt and pepper

¼ cup grapeseed oil

1 cup chopped Spanish onion

1 cup chopped leek

6 cloves garlic, chopped

2 jalapeño chiles, seeded and chopped

1½ cups red wine

1 cup coarsely grated horseradish

3 sprigs rosemary

1½ cups Chicken Stock (see Appendices)

16 small shallots

2 tablespoons olive oil

1½ tablespoons chopped fresh flat-leaf parsley

1½ pounds Yukon Gold potatoes, peeled and chopped

½ cup butter

1 cup milk, hot

½ cup plus 4 teaspoons finely grated horseradish

½ cup Red Wine Jus, hot (see Appendices)

METHOD To prepare the ribs: Preheat the oven to 350 degrees. Season the ribs with salt and pepper. Sear the ribs with the grapeseed oil in a hot roasting pan over medium-high heat for 2 to 3 minutes on each side, or until golden brown. Remove the ribs from the roasting pan and set aside.

Cook the onion, leek, garlic, and jalapeños in the roasting pan over medium-high heat for 7 to 10 minutes, or until golden brown. Add the red wine, coarsely grated horseradish, rosemary, and Chicken Stock and bring to a simmer. Return the ribs to the pan and cover with aluminum foil. Braise in the oven for 3 to 4 hours, or until the meat is fork tender. (The braising liquid may be strained, reduced, and used as a sauce.)

To prepare the shallots: Place the shallots in an ovenproof pan with the olive oil and cover with aluminum foil. Roast at 350 degrees for 1 hour, or until tender. Toss the shallots with the parsley and season to taste with salt and pepper.

To prepare the potatoes: Cook the potatoes in boiling salted water until tender. Drain and pass through a ricer. Place the potatoes in a medium bowl with the butter, ½ cup of the milk, and ½ cup of the finely grated horseradish and whip until smooth. Place in a saucepan and whisk in the remaining ½ cup milk until the mixture has a ribbon-like consistency. Season to taste with salt and pepper.

ASSEMBLY Arrange some of the shallots and ribs in the center of each plate. Spoon a ring of the horseradish potato purée around the plate. Spoon the Red Wine Jus over the ribs and sprinkle with the remaining 4 teaspoons finely grated horseradish.

Substitutions

Pork, oxtail, lamb shank

Wine Notes

An American classic, this dish is made for a classic American red wine, Merlot from California. The sweet, caramelized onion and leek are countered by the spice from the jalapeños and horseradish, and a ripe, juicy Merlot adds just the right fruit component. Pride Mountain crafts the ideal plush, big-fruit style. Martin Ray's *Diamond Mountain* from Napa Valley is a bigger, deeper wine that also works well with this course.

Dry-Aged Beef Strip Loin with Foie Gras–Oxtail Ravioli, Collard Greens, and Red Curry–Red Wine Emulsion

~~~~~~

Dry-aged beef alone is tremendous, but pairing it with a foie gras–oxtail ravioli nudges it over the edge. The presence of heady morel mushrooms with their purée, raises the bar even higher. Finally, a red curry–red wine emulsion adds notes of concentrated fruit along with playfully elegant spice to round out everything and provide a lovely lusciousness.

Serves 4

4 ounces foie gras, cleaned

Salt and pepper

1/2 cup Braised Oxtail (see Appendices)

1/4 cup diced dried apricots

8 4 by 1 1/2-inch pieces Semolina Pasta (recipe follows)

1 egg yolk, lightly beaten

1 teaspoon minced shallot

1/4 cup plus 1 tablespoon butter

26 half-free morel mushrooms, cleaned

2 cups Chicken Stock (see Appendices)

2 tablespoons red curry paste

1 cup Red Wine Jus (see Appendices)

1 1-pound dry-aged beef strip loin

1 tablespoon grapeseed oil

1 cup Braised Collard Greens, warm (recipe follows)

1/2 cup Meat Stock Reduction, hot (see Appendices)

2 teaspoons fresh thyme leaves

METHOD To prepare the ravioli: Season the foie gras with salt and pepper. Place in a hot sauté pan and cook over medium-high heat for 1 to 2 minutes on each side, or until just cooked. Dice the foie gras and place in a bowl. Add the Braised Oxtail and apricots and season with salt and pepper.

Lay 4 pieces of the pasta on a flat surface and lightly brush with the egg yolk. Spoon some of the oxtail mixture down the center of the pasta and cover with a second sheet of pasta. Firmly press the sides together and refrigerate for 30 minutes. Just prior to serving, cook the pasta in boiling salted water for 4 minutes, or until al dente. Drain the pasta and slice in half on the diagonal.

To prepare the mushrooms: Sweat the shallot in 1 tablespoon of the butter in a sauté pan over medium heat for 1 minute. Add the mushrooms and cook for 3 to 5 minutes, or until tender. Add 1 cup of Chicken Stock and cook for 1 minute, or until warm. Season to taste with salt and pepper. Purée 10 of the mushrooms with Chicken Stock until smooth. Warm the purée in a small saucepan and season with salt and pepper.

To prepare the emulsion: Place the curry paste with the remaining 1 cup Chicken Stock in a small saucepan and simmer for 10 minutes over medium heat, or until the curry paste is incorporated. Add the Red Wine Jus and simmer for 5 minutes. Whisk in the remaining 1/4 cup butter and season to taste with salt and pepper. Froth with a handheld blender just prior to serving.

To prepare the strip loin: Brush the strip loin with grapeseed oil and season with salt and pepper. Grill over medium heat for 4 minutes on each side, or until medium-rare. Let rest for 3 minutes and cut into thick slices. Season with salt and pepper.

ASSEMBLY Spoon the mushroom purée in the shape of an X on each plate. Arrange the collard greens and mushrooms in the center of each plate. Place the strip loin and 2 halves of the pasta over the collard greens. Spoon on the warm Meat Stock Reduction and the emulsion. Sprinkle with the thyme leaves and top with black pepper.

Semolina Pasta

Yield: about 1 1/2 pounds

2 cups extra-fine semolina flour

3 eggs, lightly beaten

METHOD Place the semolina flour and the eggs in the bowl of an electric mixer and mix on low speed with the paddle attachment for 3 minutes, or until the dough comes together. Form the dough into a ball and cover with plastic wrap. Refrigerate for at least 1 hour before rolling out.

Braised Collard Greens

Yield: approximately 1 1/2 cups

1/2 cup chopped bacon

4 cups loosely packed chopped collard greens

1 tablespoon brown sugar

2 tablespoons sherry wine vinegar

1/2 cup water

Salt and pepper

Cook the bacon in a medium sauté pan over medium-low heat for 5 minutes, or until the fat is rendered. Add the collard greens and cook for 3 minutes, or until wilted. Add the brown sugar, sherry wine vinegar, and water and cook over very low heat for 30 minutes, or until the greens are tender. Season to taste with salt and pepper.

Substitutions

Veal, pork, squab, salmon

Wine Notes

The strip loin and foie gras–oxtail pasta in this dish are given a red-hot kick by the curry emulsion. A red with rich fruit and toasty, slightly sweet oak is needed to tame the spice. Two reds from Washington State do the job: Delille's *Chaleur Estate* and Andrew Will Winery's *Klipsun Merlot*. Both wines are packed with ripe fruit within a well-balanced structure.

Beef Tenderloin Medallions with Ratatouille and Anchovy–Pine Nut Vinaigrette

The full flavor of the beef works perfectly with the lively ratatouille and is equally complemented by the musty, heady anchovy–pine nut vinaigrette. The ratatouille is especially explosive in flavor because all the ingredients are briefly sautéed rather than cooking them slowly together. This creates a less muddy flavor. Capers and Basil Oil provide the final whimsical, but important, flavor notes.

Serves 4

1 shallot, minced

1 cup plus 3 tablespoons olive oil

Pinch of saffron threads

2 cups peeled, seeded, and chopped tomato

1 cup finely julienned Spanish onion

5 cloves garlic, minced

½ cup finely julienned red bell pepper

½ cup finely julienned yellow bell pepper

½ cup finely julienned zucchini

½ cup finely julienned yellow squash

½ cup finely julienned eggplant

2 tablespoons fresh basil chiffonade

Salt and pepper

15 salt-packed anchovies, filleted, rinsed, and chopped

¼ cup balsamic vinegar

1 red bell pepper, chopped

¼ cup pine nuts, toasted

4 3-ounce beef tenderloin medallions

1 tablespoon grapeseed oil

¼ cup capers, rinsed

8 teaspoons Basil Oil (see Appendices)

METHOD To prepare the tomato sauce: Sweat the shallot in 1 tablespoon of the olive oil in a small sauté pan over medium-low heat for 2 minutes. Add the saffron and cook for 1 minute. Add the tomatoes and cook over medium heat for 30 minutes. Purée until smooth and pass through a fine-mesh sieve.

To prepare the ratatouille: Sauté the onion in 2 tablespoons of the olive oil in a medium sauté pan over medium heat for 5 minutes, or until caramelized. Add the garlic and cook for 1 minute. Add the julienned red and yellow bell peppers, zucchini, yellow squash, and eggplant and cook for 5 minutes, or until the vegetables are tender. Fold the tomato sauce and basil into the vegetables and season with salt and pepper.

To prepare the vinaigrette: Purée the anchovies, balsamic vinegar, the remaining 1 cup olive oil, the chopped red bell pepper, and the pine nuts until smooth. Pass through a fine-mesh sieve and season to taste with salt and pepper. Warm the vinaigrette over medium heat for 2 to 3 minutes, or until warm.

To prepare the beef: Season the beef medallions with salt and pepper. Place the medallions in a hot sauté pan with the grapeseed oil and cook over medium heat for 4 minutes on each side, or until cooked rare. Allow the meat to rest for 3 minutes before slicing in half. Season with salt and pepper.

ASSEMBLY Place some of the ratatouille in the center of each plate. Set 2 pieces of the meat over the ratatouille and sprinkle the capers around the plate. Spoon the vinaigrette and Basil Oil around the plate and top with freshly ground black pepper.

Substitutions

Chicken, veal, squab

Wine Notes

While the red and yellow bell peppers in the ratatouille are well matched by a peppery Cabernet Sauvignon from Napa Valley, for the whole dish, Cabernet Franc is the better match. The herbaceous quality of Château Simard from St. Émilion in Bordeaux is a stimulating pairing with all of the other vegetable elements and the basil.

Venison with Mole and Cashew Vinaigrette

This sturdy and full-flavored mole sauce certainly can stand up to a rich meat like venison.
The beauty of this particular mole, though, is that it is more reliant on spice than heat, and thus will
not overwhelm the meat. Also, the "heat" in the mole can easily be ratcheted up or down.
Pieces of lightly sautéed apple add a delicate sweetness and a little drizzle of cashew vinaigrette
provides a lusty richness that helps tie all of the elements together.

Serves 4

8 red pearl onions

3 tablespoons butter

2 tablespoons dried cherries

12 fresh cherries, pitted and quartered

Salt and pepper

*1 red apple, peeled and cut into
oblique wedges*

⅓ cup toasted, finely chopped cashews

1½ tablespoons rice vinegar

1½ tablespoons freshly squeezed lemon juice

2 tablespoons water

½ cup olive oil

*1 12-ounce venison tenderloin
(about 1½ inches in diameter)*

1½ tablespoons grapeseed oil

Mole (recipe follows)

Fleur de sel

¼ cup toasted, coarsely chopped cashews

*2 red Thai chiles, thinly sliced on the
diagonal*

METHOD To prepare the onion mixture:
Cook the pearl onions in boiling salted
water for 2 to 3 minutes. Drain and remove
the skins from the onions. Cut any large
onions in half. Place the onions in a sauté
pan with 2 tablespoons of the butter and
cook over medium heat for 7 minutes, or
until caramelized. Add the dried and fresh
cherries to the pan, cook for 3 minutes, and
season to taste with salt and pepper.

To prepare the apple: Sauté the apple with
the remaining 1 tablespoon butter in a
sauté pan over medium heat for 5 minutes,
or until caramelized. Season to taste with
salt and pepper.

To prepare the cashew vinaigrette: Purée the
cashews, rice vinegar, lemon juice, water,
and olive oil until smooth. Pass through a
fine-mesh sieve and season to taste with salt
and pepper. Place in a small saucepan and
warm over low heat just prior to serving.

To prepare the venison: Season the venison
with salt and pepper. Place the venison in a
hot sauté pan with the grapeseed oil and
cook over medium heat for 4 minutes on
each side, or until cooked medium. Remove
the venison from the pan, let rest for 3 minutes, and cut into four 1-inch-thick slices.

ASSEMBLY Spoon some of the Mole in the
center of each plate and top with a venison
slice. Place some of the cashew vinaigrette
at 4 spots on the plate. Arrange the onion
mixture and apple over the vinaigrette and
Mole. Season the venison with the fleur de
sel and sprinkle the chopped cashews and
Thai chile around the plate.

Mole

Yield: approximately 3 cups

2 serrano chiles, seeded and chopped

1 chipolte chile in adobo, seeded and chopped

1 ancho chile, seeded and chopped

2 tablespoons rendered bacon fat

1 cup small-diced Spanish onion

2 cloves garlic, minced

1 jalapeño chile, seeded and minced

½ cup peeled, chopped Granny Smith apple

¼ cup toasted, chopped almonds

¼ cup toasted, chopped cashews

1 tablespoon black sesame seeds

2 whole cloves

¼ teaspoon ground nutmeg

¼ teaspoon ground mace

¼ teaspoon ground cinnamon

4 dried apricots, chopped

¼ cup dried cherries

¼ cup golden raisins

1 cup Vegetable Stock (see Appendices)

2 cups Chicken Stock (see Appendices)

1 teaspoon chopped fresh oregano

2 sprigs thyme

2 ounces dark chocolate, chopped

½ cup diced brioche

METHOD Place the serrano, chipolte, and
ancho chiles in a large cast-iron skillet and
cook over medium heat for 10 to 15 minutes, or until black. Add the bacon fat,
onion, garlic, jalapeño, and apple and cook
for 10 minutes, or until the apple is tender.
Add the almonds, cashews, sesame seeds,
cloves, nutmeg, mace, and cinnamon and
cook for 7 to 10 minutes, or until the nuts
smell toasty. Add the dried apricots, cherries, and raisins and cook for 10 minutes.
Add the Vegetable Stock, Chicken Stock,
oregano, and thyme and cook for 15 minutes. Add the chocolate and the brioche and
cook for 20 minutes. Purée the Mole until
smooth, pass through a fine-mesh sieve,
and season to taste with salt and pepper.
(The Mole can be prepared 3 days in
advance and stored in the refrigerator.)

Substitutions

Beef, chicken, lobster, pork

Wine Notes

Chocolate, nuts, and sweet dried fruit are
flavor descriptors often attributed to Cabernet Sauvignon, and indeed, such a red
works with this dish. Young, opulent wines
like the Napa Valley Cabernets of Bryant
Family, Araujo, and Dalla Valle absorb the
spice of the chiles and envelop the rich
venison with additional ripe fruit.

Roasted Scottish Hare Loin with Green Garlic, Braised Tiny Leeks, and Caper-Cornichon–Egg White Vinaigrette

For hare, a full-flavored meat, this is a fairly light preparation that allows its texture and flavor to shine through. Green garlic and braised tiny leeks provide texture and an appropriate earthiness. The vinaigrette, however, imparts the life and vitality that help to temper the prominence of the meat. A drizzle of meat reduction ties the ingredients together.

Serves 4

20 small pieces green garlic

3 tablespoons rendered bacon fat

Salt and pepper

12 tiny leeks, halved lengthwise

2 tablespoons butter

1 cup Vegetable Stock (see Appendices)

1 cup olive oil

2 tablespoons sherry wine vinegar

2 hard-boiled eggs, yolks discarded and whites cut into brunoise

1/4 cup tiny capers, rinsed

1/4 cup brunoise-cut cornichon

1/4 cup brunoise-cut green olive

1/4 cup brunoise-cut carrot, parboiled

2 teaspoons chopped fresh chervil

2 teaspoons chopped fresh chives

2 teaspoons chopped fresh flat-leaf parsley

1/2 teaspoon chopped fresh sage

4 Scottish hare tenderloins (about 12 ounces total)

1 tablespoon grapeseed oil

1/2 cup hot Veal Stock Reduction, hot (see Appendices)

METHOD To prepare the green garlic: Preheat the oven to 350 degrees. Place the garlic in a small roasting pan with the bacon fat and roast in the oven for 30 to 45 minutes, or until tender. Remove the garlic from the pan and season to taste with salt and pepper.

To prepare the leeks: Place the leeks, butter, and Vegetable Stock in a small saucepan and simmer over low heat for 10 minutes, or until the leeks are tender. Remove the leeks from the liquid and season to taste with salt and pepper.

To prepare the vinaigrette: Place the olive oil in a medium bowl and whisk in the sherry wine vinegar. Fold in the egg white, capers, cornichon, green olive, carrot, chervil, chives, parsley, and sage. Season to taste with salt and pepper.

To prepare the hare: Season the hare tenderloins with salt and pepper. Place in a hot sauté pan with the grapeseed oil and cook over medium-high heat for 2 minutes on each side, or until cooked medium. Let rest for 3 minutes and then halve lengthwise on the diagonal. Season with salt and pepper.

ASSEMBLY Arrange some of the tiny leeks in the center of each plate and lean 2 halves of the hare on top of the leeks. Arrange some of the green garlic around the plate and spoon the vinaigrette over the hare and around the plate. Spoon the Veal Stock Reduction around the plate and top with freshly ground black pepper.

Substitutions

Rabbit, beef, chicken

Wine Notes

A California Red Meritage with a pronounced Cabernet Franc influence is a good choice for this dish. The richness of the red embraces the full-flavored hare meat. *Maya* from Napa Valley's Dalla Valle is one example in which the herbaceousness of Cabernet Franc handles the green elements of caper, olives, cornichons, and garlic.

Braised Beef Cheeks with Celery Root Purée, Hedgehog Mushrooms, Gnocchi Galette, and Sage

Although the elements of this preparation are strewn about in a free-form way, and the dish appears to be quite casual, the flavor and texture combination is profound. The braised beef cheek meat may be the star of the plate, but it is richly enhanced by the other elements. Elegant, meaty hedgehog mushrooms provide the perfect earthiness, and a creamy galette of gnocchi adds a sensual note. A purée of celery root delivers a richness, and a drizzle of the braising liquid weaves everything together. To go berserk, I suppose one could place a nice-sized piece of seared foie gras right on top of the galette and maybe add some black truffle, too.

Serves 4

1 cup chopped celery root

1 sprig thyme

5 tablespoons butter

Salt and pepper

Grapeseed oil for deep-frying

24 tiny fresh sage leaves

1 tablespoon minced shallot

1 1/2 cups hedgehog mushrooms, cleaned

1 tablespoon fresh flat-leaf parsley chiffonade

1 teaspoon fresh thyme leaves

1 cup loosely packed celery leaves

Crispy Semolina Gnocchi (recipe follows)

Braised Beef Cheeks, braising liquid reserved (see Appendices)

4 teaspoons olive oil

2 teaspoons fresh sage chiffonade

METHOD To prepare the celery root: Place the celery root and thyme sprig in a small saucepan and cover with water. Simmer over medium heat for 15 minutes, or until tender. Discard the thyme sprig. Purée the celery root with just enough of the cooking liquid to make a thin purée. Whisk in 2 tablespoons of the butter and season to taste with salt and pepper.

To prepare the sage leaves: Pour grapeseed oil to a depth of ½ inch in a small shallow pan over medium-high heat until very hot. Add the sage leaves and cook for 15 to 30 seconds, or until crispy. Blot on paper towels and season with salt.

To prepare the mushrooms: Cook the shallot with 2 tablespoons of the butter in a small sauté pan over medium-low heat for 2 to 3 minutes, or until translucent. Add the mushrooms and sauté for 3 to 4 minutes, or until tender. Add the parsley and thyme and season to taste with salt and pepper.

To prepare the celery leaves: Wilt the celery leaves with the remaining 1 tablespoon butter in a hot sauté pan over medium heat for 1 minute. Season with salt and pepper.

ASSEMBLY Place some of the wilted celery leaves in the center of each plate and top with a crispy gnocchi. Spoon some of the celery root purée in a ring around the plate. Arrange the beef cheeks and mushrooms at 4 points around the plate. Spoon some of the braising liquid and drizzle the olive oil around the plate. Sprinkle the fried sage leaves and sage chiffonade around the plate and top with freshly ground black pepper.

Crispy Semolina Gnocchi

Yield: 1 8-inch square pan

2 1/2 pounds Idaho potatoes, boiled and riced

1 egg

Salt and pepper

1 tablespoon finely chopped arugula

3/4 cup semolina flour

1/2 to 3/4 cup all-purpose flour

2 tablespoons butter

METHOD Place the hot riced potato in a large bowl. Work the egg yolk into the potato with a wooden spoon, and season with salt and pepper. Add the arugula, semolina flour, and ½ cup of the all-purpose flour. Work the mixture together with a wooden spoon or your fingers, adding only enough of the remaining ¼ cup all-purpose flour as needed to allow the mixture to come together. Firmly press the gnocchi into an 8-inch square pan. Cover with plastic wrap and refrigerate for at least 1 hour.

Using a 2-inch round ring cutter, cut the gnocchi into 4 disks (the extra gnocchi can be refrigerated for 2 days). Place the disks in a hot sauté pan with the butter and cook over medium heat for 2 minutes on each side, or until golden brown and crispy.

Substitutions

Oxtail, veal, lamb

Wine Notes

There are so many delights for the senses in this dish: crispy potato gnocchi, aromatic fried sage, and the melt-in-your-mouth beef cheeks. An elegant, mature Bordeaux would be a treat for this course, echoing the meatiness and supple textures. Château Léoville-Las-Cases and Château Ducru-Beaucaillou from Saint Julien are favorites at the restaurant.

Axis Venison Rack with Braised Bok Choy, Black Truffles, and Roasted Garnet Yam

The flavors in this dish are masculine and full, but at the same time, the preparation comes across as rather light. The rich flavor of the venison rack is ideally offset by the clean, just-crunchy braised bok choy. Heady black truffle is the extravagant note, while the garnet yams add a mellow sweetness. Chanterelle mushrooms with their purée provide a regal earthiness, and the reduction sauce harmonizes the dish.

Serves 4

1 small garnet yam, peeled

2 tablespoons rendered duck fat

4 cloves garlic, quartered

Salt and pepper

4 heads baby bok choy

3 tablespoons butter

2 cups Vegetable Stock (see Appendices)

1 black truffle, thinly sliced

1 tablespoon minced shallot

3 cups chanterelle mushrooms, cleaned

¼ teaspoon rice vinegar

1 axis venison rack with 8 chops, frenched

1 tablespoon grapeseed oil

½ cup Venison Stock Reduction, hot (see Appendices)

METHOD To prepare the yam: Preheat the oven to 400 degrees. Cut the yam into bite-sized oblique pieces and place in a roasting pan with the duck fat and garlic. Roast for 30 to 40 minutes, or until caramelized and tender. Season to taste with salt and pepper. Purée half of the yam with enough water to create a smooth purée. Season to taste with salt and pepper. Reheat just prior to serving.

To prepare the bok choy: Place the bok choy in a sauté pan with 1 tablespoon of the butter and the Vegetable Stock and cook over medium heat for 5 to 7 minutes, or until tender. Remove the bok choy and reserve the cooking liquid. Cut 4 grooves in the bok choy starting about ½ inch from the base and going through the top of the leaves. Insert the truffle slices into the grooves and season to taste with salt and pepper. Warm the bok choy in the reserved cooking liquid just prior to serving.

To prepare the mushrooms: Sweat the shallot in the remaining 2 tablespoons butter in a medium sauté pan over medium heat for 30 seconds. Add the mushrooms and cook for 5 to 7 minutes, or until tender. Stir in the rice vinegar and remove from the heat. Purée half of the mushrooms with enough water to create a smooth purée. Season to taste with salt and pepper. Season the remaining mushrooms with salt and pepper. Warm the mushrooms and purée just prior to serving.

To prepare the venison: Preheat the oven to 400 degrees. Season the venison with salt and pepper. Sear the venison in a hot roasting pan with the grapeseed oil over medium-high heat for 2 to 3 minutes on each side, or until golden brown. Roast in the oven for 15 minutes, or until cooked medium-rare. Let rest for 5 minutes. Cut the rack into 8 chops and season to taste with salt and pepper.

ASSEMBLY Spoon the mushroom and yam purées in the center of each plate in a horizontal line. Place a piece of the bok choy at the top of the plate and arrange the mushrooms and yams around the plate. Lean 2 venison chops over the bok choy. Spoon the Venison Stock Reduction over the chops and around the plate. Top with freshly ground black pepper.

Substitutions

Beef, lamb, pork, scallops

Wine Notes

This dish provides a great opportunity to showcase a serious, complex, aged red. A Super Tuscan displaying great density of fruit like Tenuta San Guido's Cabernet Sauvignon–based Sassacaia, from a great vintage, should be brought up from the cellar for a special treat. It's a decadent pairing with the earthy black truffle, sweet roasted yam, and the rich duck confit fat that round out the flavors of the dish.

Date-Crusted Venison Tenderloin with Salsify-Strewn Quinoa and Ginger-Infused Venison Jus

Although this dish has hearty flavors it is actually fairly light.
The cardamom-flavored date preserve provides a fabulous counterpoint to the robust meat.
The quinoa and the chanterelles help to anchor the dish with earthy notes, yet their
flavors echo the overall theme of lightness. Salsify appears both as pieces strewn in the grain
and in the form of a delicate purée, its presence adding the perfect flavor note of elegance.

Serves 4

3 stalks salsify, peeled and cut into 2-inch-long pieces

2 cups milk

Salt and pepper

3 tablespoons butter

1/2 cup julienned bacon

1/4 cup brunoise-cut carrot

1/4 cup brunoise-cut celery root

1 cup chanterelle mushrooms, cleaned

1 cup cooked quinoa

1 teaspoon sherry wine vinegar

3 cardamom pods, seeds removed and finely crushed

1/2 cup dry white wine

1 green Thai chile, seeded and finely chopped

1 cup chopped dates

1 1-pound venison tenderloin

1 tablespoon grapeseed oil

1 head broccoli rabe, stems trimmed and blanched

1 tablespoon minced shallot

1/2 cup Venison Stock Reduction (see Appendices)

1 teaspoon minced fresh ginger

2 tablespoons Preserved Ginger (see Appendices)

2 teaspoons fresh sage chiffonade

METHOD To prepare the salsify: Place the salsify pieces in a saucepan and cover with the milk. Simmer the salsify for 10 to 12 minutes, or until tender. Remove the salsify from the milk. Purée one-third of the salsify with 1/3 cup of the milk until smooth and season to taste with salt and pepper. Cut the remaining salsify in half lengthwise and sauté with 1 tablespoon of the butter in a sauté pan over medium-high heat for 3 minutes, or until golden brown. Season to taste with salt and pepper.

To prepare the quinoa: Cook the bacon in a hot sauté pan over medium heat for 3 to 4 minutes, or until the fat has been rendered. Add the carrot and celery root and cook for 2 minutes. Add the mushrooms and cook for 5 minutes, or until the mushrooms are tender. Add the quinoa and cook for 2 minutes, or until warm. Add the sherry wine vinegar and salsify pieces and season to taste with salt and pepper.

To prepare the venison: Toast the cardamom in a small sauté pan over medium heat for 2 minutes. Add the white wine, Thai chile, and dates and cook for 5 minutes. Mash the date mixture with a fork and season to taste with salt.

Brush the venison with the grapeseed oil and season with salt and pepper. Grill over medium heat for 4 minutes on each side, or until cooked medium-rare. Remove from the grill, cover with the date purée, and let rest for 3 minutes. Cut into 1/2-inch-thick slices and season with salt and pepper.

To prepare the broccoli rabe: Sweat the shallot with the remaining 2 tablespoons butter over medium heat for 2 minutes. Add the broccoli rabe and sauté for 5 minutes, or until hot. Season to taste with salt and pepper.

To prepare the reduction sauce: Place the Venison Stock Reduction in a small saucepan with the fresh ginger and simmer over medium heat for 5 minutes. Strain through a fine-mesh sieve and season to taste with salt and pepper.

ASSEMBLY Spoon the Venison Stock Reduction and the salsify purée in the center of each plate in a ticktacktoe formation. Place some of the quinoa mixture and broccoli rabe in the center of each plate. Arrange 2 slices of venison over the quinoa and sprinkle the Preserved Ginger and sage over the venison and around the plate. Spoon some of the Venison Stock Reduction over the venison and top with freshly ground black pepper.

Substitutions

Beef, squab, salmon

Wine Notes

From the Ribera del Duero in Spain, Vega Sicilia crafts luxurious Cabernet Sauvignon–based reds *Unico* and *Valbuena* with jammy, fleshy fruit and generous structures. These elegantly styled wines meet the challenge of the peppery, almost tannic broccoli rabe with dense, dark fruits and echo the rich ginger in the reduction with sweet, spicy notes.

Braised Oxtail, Savoy Cabbage, and Yukon Gold Potato Tart with Tiny Squash and Their Blossoms and Young Thyme

A preparation like this is absolutely soul satisfying. The meltaway oxtail meat is layered with ever-so-slightly astringent braised savoy cabbage and pieces of earthy Yukon Gold potato, the entirety of which is wrapped in flaky, buttery pastry. The result is a dish of humble ingredients that reaches lofty heights. Delicate squash pieces help cut into the richness of the meat, and young thyme acts as a clean, refreshing foil for the pastry.

Serves 4

2 cups loosely packed spinach

1 shallot, minced

4 tablespoons butter

Salt and pepper

4 cups coarsely chopped loosely packed savoy cabbage

1 teaspoon coarsely ground caraway seeds

Pâte Brisée (recipe follows)

1½ cups Braised Oxtail, braising liquid reserved (see Appendices)

1 Yukon Gold potato, baked, peeled, and cut into/-inch-thick disks

1 egg, lightly beaten

8 squash blossoms, pistils removed

4 baby zucchini

4 baby gooseneck yellow squashes

24 sprigs young thyme

METHOD To prepare the spinach: Quickly sauté the spinach and shallot with 1 tablespoon of the butter in a hot sauté pan over medium heat for 3 to 4 minutes, or until wilted. Season to taste with salt and pepper and cool to room temperature.

To prepare the savoy cabbage: Place the savoy cabbage, caraway seeds, and 2 tablespoons of the butter in a medium saucepan. Add enough water to barely cover the cabbage and cook over medium-low heat for 15 minutes, or until tender. Drain the cabbage and set aside.

To assemble the tarts: Preheat the oven to 375 degrees. Roll out the Pâte Brisée dough ⅛ inch thick on a lightly floured surface.

Cut out four 7-inch circles and four 3-inch circles from the dough. Place 4 ring molds, each 2½ inches wide by 1½ inches high, on a parchment-lined sheet pan and press a large dough circle into each mold, allowing for some overhang. Place 2 tablespoons of the oxtail meat in the bottom of the tarts and layer with some of the savoy cabbage. Repeat this process a second time. Place a layer of potato over the cabbage and top with a layer of the spinach. Lay the smaller circle of tart dough on top of the spinach and seal the edges. Refrigerate for 30 minutes. Lightly brush the top of the tart with the egg. Sprinkle salt on the top of each tart and bake for 35 minutes, or until golden brown. Let sit for 5 minutes, remove from the rings, and cut in half.

To prepare the squash blossoms: Stuff each squash blossom with 1 tablespoon of the braised oxtail meat. Place in a steamer and warm for 3 to 4 minutes, or until hot.

To prepare the zucchini and yellow squashes: Cut the zucchini and squashes into ¼-inch-thick pieces on the diagonal. Sauté the vegetables with the remaining 1 tablespoon butter in a small sauté pan for 3 to 4 minutes, or until tender. Season to taste with salt and pepper.

ASSEMBLY Place 2 halves of the tart in the center of each plate. Place a squash blossom on each side of the tart, and arrange the zucchini and squash pieces around the plate. Spoon the warm reduced braising liquid around the plate and sprinkle with the thyme sprigs.

Pâte Brisée

Yield: 1 9-inch pie crust

1¼ cups flour

2 tablespoons sugar

¾ teaspoon salt

⅔ cup cold butter, cubed

1 egg yolk

3 tablespoons ice water

METHOD Place the flour, sugar, salt, and butter in the bowl of an electric mixer. Using the paddle attachment, mix on low until the ingredients are combined and the texture is coarse. Add the egg yolk and water all at once and mix on low speed until the dough just comes together. Work the dough into a ball and wrap in plastic wrap. Refrigerate for 30 minutes, or until ready to use.

Substitutions

Lamb, beef, veal

Wine Notes

The rich, stewlike oxtail and buttery Pâte Brisée are punctuated by the vegetable elements of squash and spinach. A mature Chilean red, particularly one that is Cabernet Sauvignon based, is an ideal match. Don Melchor from Concha y Toro matures into a velvety, rich red with signature minty menthol tones that merge with the vibrant notes of the thyme and caraway. Another wine to try is the Chilean Cabernet Almaviva, a collaboration between Concha y Toro and the Rothschilds.

Braised Lamb Shank with
Horseradish–Celery Root Purée and Red Lentils

Slowly braised lamb shank is a favorite treat of mine. Here, the rich braised
meat is made even more extravagant by a bed of buttery red lentils.
The clean bite of horseradish incorporated into puréed celery root provides the
perfect poignant, yet contained, bite to contrast against this luscious meat.
This preparation could be made even more robust if sautéed mushrooms were added.

Serves 4

1 cup chopped celery root

⅓ cup chopped horseradish

1½ cups milk

Salt and pepper

1 cup Pickling Juice (see Appendices)

½ cup small-diced celery root

1 carrot, cut into large pieces

1 small Spanish onion, cut into large pieces

1 stalk celery, cut into large pieces

2 tablespoons butter

¾ cup red lentils

2 cups Chicken Stock (see Appendices)

2 tablespoons chopped fresh chives

*Braised Lamb Shank, reduced braising
liquid reserved (see Appendices)*

*16 pieces Roasted Garlic cloves
(see Appendices)*

1 tablespoon long-cut fresh chives

METHOD To prepare the celery root purée:
Place the chopped celery root, horseradish,
and milk in a medium saucepan and simmer over medium heat for 20 minutes, or

until the celery root is tender. Drain the
milk from the pan, reserving about ⅔ cup.
Purée the celery root and horseradish with
just enough of the reserved milk to form a
thick purée. Pass through a fine-mesh sieve
and season to taste with salt and pepper.

To prepare the pickled celery root: Place
the Pickling Juice in a saucepan with the
small-diced celery root. Simmer over
medium heat for 5 minutes, or until tender.
Remove the celery root from the liquid just
prior to serving.

To prepare the lentils: Cook the carrot,
onion, and celery in the butter in a small
saucepan over medium heat for 5 minutes,
or until they just begin to brown. Add the
lentils and cook for 3 minutes. Add the
Chicken Stock and simmer for 1 hour, or
until the lentils are tender. Remove the big
pieces of carrot, onion, and celery and discard. Season the lentils to taste with salt
and pepper. Fold in the chopped chives.

To prepare the lamb: Cut the Braised Lamb
Shank into 2-inch pieces and warm in the

oven if necessary. Brush the lamb shank
with some of the reduced braising liquid
and season to taste with salt and pepper.

ASSEMBLY Spoon the lentils and pickled
celery root in the center of each plate.
Arrange 3 pieces of the lamb shank over
the lentils and place 4 Roasted Garlic
cloves around the plate. Spoon the celery
root purée and reduced braising liquid
around the plate and sprinkle with the
chives.

Substitutions

Veal, pork, beef

Wine Notes

Tangy pickled celery root interjects some
exciting brightness to the comfortingly
dark, rich braised shank, roasted garlic, and
earthy lentils. While many Old World reds
would be suitable, a mature Brunello di
Montalcino from Castello Banfi, or if you
can procure one, a bottle of *Sugarille* from
Angelo Gaja, will be a rare pleasure.

Varietal Meat

Varietal Meat

Veal Brains with Three Beets
and Thyme Leaves

Veal brains, when properly cooked, are creamy and meltingly soft.
When fried or sautéed over medium-high heat, however, they gain the bonus of a crispy exterior.
It's then that gloriousness is achieved. Here, sweet beets are not only the ideal flavor match
for the brains, utterly highlighting their delicacy, but also provide a wonderful textural contrast.
Veal juice and thyme are all that is needed to finish the dish.

Serves 4

12 candy cane beets

2 large red beets

1 large yellow beet

2 tablespoons olive oil

Salt and pepper

6 sprigs thyme

3 tablespoons butter

1 pound veal brains, cut into
1 to 1 1/2-ounce pieces

1 cup flour

3 tablespoons grapeseed oil

Fleur de sel

1 teaspoon fresh thyme leaves

4 teaspoons Herb Oil (see Appendices)

1/3 cup Veal Stock Reduction, hot
(see Appendices)

METHOD To prepare the beet chips: Preheat the oven to 250 degrees. Peel and thinly slice 4 of the candy cane beets. Lay the large slices from the middle of the beets on a silpat-lined or nonstick sheet pan and bake for 1 hour, or until the beet slices are dry. Remove the beet chips while warm and cool on a plate. Store in an airtight container until ready to use.

To prepare the beets: Preheat the oven to 350 degrees. Rub the remaining 8 candy cane beets and the large red and yellow beets with olive oil and season with salt and pepper. Place the large beets in an ovenproof pan with 4 sprigs of the thyme, making sure the red and yellow beets do not touch each other. Place the remaining 8 candy cane beets in an ovenproof pan with the remaining 2 sprigs thyme. Roast the large beets for 2 hours, or until tender. Roast the candy cane beets for 1 hour, or until tender.

Peel all the beets, making sure the yellow and red beets do not touch. Cut the large red and yellow beets into thin wedges and season to taste with salt and pepper. Cut the candy cane beets in half and season to taste with salt and pepper. Purée one-half of the red beets with enough water to create a smooth purée. Warm the beet purée in a small saucepan, whisk in the butter, and season to taste with salt and pepper.

To prepare the veal brains: Season the veal brains with salt and pepper and lightly coat with the flour. Place the veal brains in a hot sauté pan with the grapeseed oil and cook over medium-high heat for 3 to 4 minutes

on each side, or until golden brown. Remove to paper towels, blot off any excess oil, and season with fleur de sel.

ASSEMBLY Spoon the red beet purée in the center of each plate in a zigzag manner. Arrange some of the red, yellow, and candy cane beets in the center of each plate. Place a few of the veal brain pieces over the beets and insert 2 dried beet chips in between the veal brain pieces. Sprinkle the thyme leaves over the plate and spoon the Herb Oil and Veal Stock Reduction around the plate.

Substitutions

Veal sweetbreads, chicken, beef

Wine Notes

A lively sparkling wine with its cleansing effect is the match for this dish, as it provides a textural contrast for the custardlike brains and the sweet roasted beets. Although a crisp Blanc de Blancs like that bottled by Schramsberg in Napa Valley achieves the desired effect, a more exciting match is a red grape–dominated sparkler. The *Grand Cuvée* from Krug, with its full body and toasty character, is a treat.

Veal Sweetbreads with Crayfish, Baby Watercress, Artichokes, and Shellfish Emulsion

This is a truly great combination of flavors and textures. The sweetbreads are crispy on the outside and soft and creamy on the inside. The crayfish are sweet and succulent, and the artichokes, appearing two ways, are both toothsome and crispy. The elements are sauced with a shellfish emulsion that subtly reinforces the flavor of the crayfish. Pieces of watercress nicely cut into the other ingredients to help keep all the flavors in balance.

Serves 4

3 cups Shellfish Stock (see Appendices)

3 tablespoons butter

Salt and pepper

20 medium crayfish, cooked

1 tablespoon chopped fresh flat-leaf parsley

3 tablespoons olive oil

3 tablespoons freshly squeezed lemon juice

3 large artichoke bottoms, stem attached

Grapeseed oil for deep-frying

1 cup dry white wine

4 sprigs thyme

4 Braised Sweetbreads nuggets (see Appendices)

¼ cup flour

2 tablespoons grapeseed oil

4 tiny purple potatoes, cooked and cut into small wedges

½ cup loosely packed baby watercress

1 teaspoon finely julienned lemon zest

4 teaspoons Shellfish Oil (see Appendices)

METHOD To prepare the shellfish emulsion: Cook the Shellfish Stock in a saucepan over medium heat for 45 minutes, or until reduced to 1½ cups. Reserve 2 tablespoons for the crayfish vinaigrette. Whisk in the butter and season to taste with salt and pepper. Froth with a handheld blender just prior to serving.

To prepare the vinaigrette: Toss the crayfish with the parsley, olive oil, 2 tablespoons of the lemon juice, and the reserved Shellfish Stock and season to taste with salt and pepper. Warm just prior to serving.

To prepare the artichokes: Thinly slice one of the artichoke bottoms. Pour grapeseed oil to a depth of 1 inch in a deep frying pan and place over high heat. Deep-fry the artichoke slices in the hot oil until golden brown and crispy. Blot on paper towels and season with salt. Rub the remaining 2 artichokes with the remaining 1 tablespoon of the lemon juice. Place in a steamer with the white wine and thyme. Steam the artichokes for 6 to 10 minutes, or until tender. Remove from the steamer and cut into bite-sized wedges. Season to taste with salt and pepper and toss with 2 tablespoons of the vinaigrette.

To prepare the sweetbreads: Season the sweetbreads with salt and pepper and dust lightly with the flour. Place the sweetbreads in a hot sauté pan with the grapeseed oil and cook over high heat for 2 minutes on each side, or until golden brown and crispy. Remove from the pan and blot on paper towels. Cut each nugget into 4 pieces and season to taste with salt and pepper.

ASSEMBLY Arrange the steamed artichoke pieces, sweetbreads, potato pieces, and watercress in the center of each plate. Spoon the crayfish vinaigrette around the plate and sprinkle with the lemon zest. Spoon some of the shellfish emulsion around the plate and sprinkle with the fried artichoke chips. Drizzle the Shellfish Oil around the plate.

Substitutions

Chicken, pork

Wine Notes

From the Wachau district in Austria, Nikolaihof's Steiner Hund Riesling Smaragd is a dry, yet full-bodied, high-toned white that meets the challenge of artichokes and lemon. The mineral component of the wine resounds nicely with the crayfish and balances the richness of the sweetbreads. The peppery watercress also finishes well with the bright acidity of the Riesling.

Braised Veal Tongue with Crayfish, Sweet Corn Emulsion, and Tiny Sage Leaves

*This combination of ultratender veal tongue and rich, succulent crayfish is made even
more extraordinary with the sweet notes provided by the corn kernels and corn emulsion.
Wilted spinach and asparagus pieces help to cut into the other ingredients, thereby acting as a significant
counterpoint in an otherwise opulent dish. Small sage leaves add a pleasant peppery bite.*

Serves 4

8 ears corn, husks removed

1 Spanish onion, chopped

2 quarts water

2 tablespoons freshly squeezed lemon juice

Salt and pepper

8½ tablespoons butter

¾ cup corn kernels

2 tablespoons minced shallot

2 cups loosely packed baby spinach

2 teaspoons sherry wine vinegar

20 crayfish, cleaned and deveined

¼ cup Shellfish Oil (see Appendices)

1 Braised Veal Tongue (recipe follows)

*16 asparagus tips, parboiled and quartered
lengthwise*

2 teaspoons tiny fresh sage leaves

METHOD To prepare the corn emulsion:
Remove the kernels from the ears of corn
and place the kernels, cobs, and onion in a
large saucepan. Cover with the water and
simmer over medium heat for 1 hour.
Strain through a fine-mesh sieve and
return the liquid to the saucepan. Simmer
over medium heat for 40 minutes, or until
reduced to 2 cups. Add 1 tablespoon of the
lemon juice and season to taste with salt
and pepper. Whisk in 5½ tablespoons of the
butter and froth with a handheld blender
just prior to serving.

To prepare the vegetables: Sauté the ¾ cup
corn kernels with 1 tablespoon of the butter
over medium heat for 4 minutes, or until
tender. Season to taste with salt and pepper.

Sweat 1 tablespoon of the shallot with
1 tablespoon of the butter in a sauté pan
over medium heat for 1 minute. Add the
spinach and sherry wine vinegar and cook
for 2 to 3 minutes, or until the spinach is
barely wilted. Season to taste with salt and
pepper.

To prepare the crayfish: Sauté the crayfish
with the remaining 1 tablespoon butter and
the shallot and cook over medium heat for
3 minutes, or until barely cooked. Add the
remaining 1 tablespoon lemon juice and
2 tablespoons of the Shellfish Oil and season to taste with salt and pepper.

ASSEMBLY Slice the Braised Veal Tongue
into ¼-inch-thick slices and season with
salt and pepper. Place some of the wilted
spinach in the center of each plate and
arrange 3 slices of the veal tongue over the
spinach. Arrange 5 of the crayfish and
some of the corn kernels and asparagus tips
around the plate. Spoon the sweet corn
emulsion around the plate and drizzle the
remaining 2 tablespoons Shellfish Oil
around the plate. Sprinkle the sage leaves
around the plate and top with freshly
ground black pepper.

Braised Veal Tongue

Yield: 1 tongue

1 veal tongue

Salt and pepper

2 tablespoons grapeseed oil

3 large carrots, cut into ¾-inch-thick slices

1½ cups chopped Spanish onion

2 leeks, chopped

2 quarts Beef Stock (see Appendices)

1 teaspoon peppercorns

1 bulb garlic, halved

8 sprigs thyme

2 bay leaves

1 cup sherry

2 sprigs rosemary

METHOD Preheat the oven to 250 degrees.
Season the tongue with salt and pepper.
Sear with the grapeseed oil in a hot braising pan over medium-high heat for 3 minutes on each side, or until golden brown.
Remove the tongue from the pan. Add the
carrots, onion, and leeks and cook for 5 to 7
minutes, or until golden brown. Return the
tongue to the pan and add the Beef Stock,
peppercorns, garlic, thyme, bay leaves,
sherry, and rosemary. Bring the mixture to
a simmer, cover, and braise in the oven for
4 to 5 hours, or until tender. Remove the
tongue from the liquid, cool, and peel off
the skin.

Substitutions

Roast beef, beef tenderloin, veal

Wine Notes

While the corn, veal tongue, and sweet-
fleshed crayfish find a friend in dry Chenin
Blanc, the white varietal has a difficult
time with the spinach and asparagus.
Choose instead a leaner, mineral-focused
White Burgundy such as Chassagne-
Montrachet *Les Vergers* from Guy Amiot.
Cru Chablis, *Valmur* or *Les Clos*, from a tra-
ditionalist producer like Raveneau will also
be rewarding.

Braised Veal Heart "Carpaccio" with Preserved Carrots and Herb Vinaigrette

*A great way to serve veal heart, after slowly braising it, is to chill it down
and then slice it paper-thin. The meat is rich, succulent, and full of flavor.
It only needs the slightest accent to push it over the edge. Here, preserved carrot, pearl
onion pieces, strands of lightly sweetened kumquat, and an herb vinaigrette make the
meat come alive. In all, it is a dish exploding with flavor and at the same time quite light.*

Serves 4

1 veal heart

Salt and pepper

1 tablespoon grapeseed oil

1 1/2 cups chopped carrot

1 1/2 cups chopped celery

2 cups chopped Spanish onion

1 cup chopped leek

1 cup red wine

4 cloves garlic

2 bay leaves

4 sprigs thyme

2 quarts Chicken Stock (see Appendices)

2 burgundy carrots, peeled

4 round carrots, peeled

1 cup Pickling Juice (see Appendices)

4 red pearl onions, peeled and sliced into thin rings

4 kumquats

1/3 cup sugar

6 tablespoons plus 1/4 cup water

1/2 cup peeled, diced McIntosh apple

12 fresh chives, blanched and chopped

1/4 cup firmly packed fresh flat-leaf parsley leaves, blanched, shocked, and chopped

1/3 cup olive oil

1 tablespoon freshly squeezed lemon juice

1/4 cup loosely packed micro chervil sprouts

Fleur de sel

METHOD To prepare the veal heart: Soak the veal heart in salted water overnight in the refrigerator. Remove and run under cold water for 5 minutes.

Preheat the oven to 300 degrees. Cut the veal heart into 3 pieces, cut away all the larger veins, and trim the excess fat from the outside. Season the heart pieces with salt and pepper. Sear the heart pieces with the grapeseed oil in a roasting pan over high heat for 3 minutes on each side, or until golden brown. Remove the veal heart, add the chopped carrot, celery, onion, and leek, and cook for 10 minutes, or until caramelized. Deglaze with the red wine and add the garlic cloves, bay leaves, and thyme. Return the veal heart pieces to the pan and cover with the Chicken Stock. Cover the roasting pan with aluminum foil and roast for 4 hours, or until tender. Cool the pieces in the braising liquid and refrigerate until cold. Cut the veal heart into paper-thin slices and season to taste with salt and pepper. (The extra braised veal heart can be frozen whole.)

To prepare the carrots and pearl onions: Thinly slice the burgundy carrots into long, wide strips. Thinly cut the round carrots into 1/16-inch-thick slices. Place 1/2 cup of the Pickling Juice in a small saucepan and bring to a simmer. Add the round carrot slices and cook for 3 minutes, or until tender. Remove the carrot slices and add the burgundy carrots. Cook the burgundy carrots for 3 minutes, or until tender, then drain. Place the remaining 1/2 cup Pickling Juice in a small saucepan, add the pearl onion slices, and cook over medium heat for 4 minutes, or until tender. Cool the onion slices in the liquid and drain.

To prepare the kumquats: Blanch the kumquats in boiling water for 3 minutes. Repeat this process 3 times. Place the kumquats in a saucepan with the sugar and 6 tablespoons of the water and cook over medium-low heat for 10 minutes. Remove the kumquats, cut them in half, and discard the pulp and seeds. Julienne the kumquats and store in the cooking liquid until ready to serve.

To prepare the apple: Place the diced apple in a saucepan with the remaining 1/4 cup water. Cook the apple over medium heat for 10 minutes, or until tender. Cool to room temperature and drain any excess liquid. Season to taste with salt and pepper.

To prepare the herb vinaigrette: Purée the chives, parsley, olive oil, and lemon juice until smooth. Season with salt and pepper.

ASSEMBLY Drizzle the herb vinaigrette around the plate. Place 5 slices of the veal heart around the plate. Roll up the burgundy carrots and place them around the plate with the round carrots, pearl onions, apple pieces, and julienned kumquat. Sprinkle the chervil sprouts around the plate. Season with the fleur de sel.

Substitutions

Roast beef, beef tenderloin, chicken

Wine Notes

The veal heart and gently sweet carrots provide the density for the dish, while the lemony herb vinaigrette and zingy kumquat provide the levity. A wine that will envelop the flavors and textures from both sides of the spectrum is needed. Chassagne-Montrachet, of the premier cru vineyards *Les Vergers* or *Les Chaumées* from Colin-Deleger, embraces all of the flavors while finishing on a high note that leaves you wanting more.

Foie Gras Five Ways

If foie gras served by itself is a great treat, then offering it up five ways is truly spectacular.
Here, it is seared, prepared in a terrine, cured, made into "ice cream," and poached to make custard.
Overwhelming perhaps, but sometimes an occasion calls for just that. Any one of these preparations
can stand on its own, too, and would be a lovely way to start a meal.

Serves 12

2 blood oranges, peeled and cut into sections

2 oranges, peeled and cut into sections

1/3 grapefruit, peeled and cut into sections

1/3 Oroblanco, peeled and cut into sections

1 tablespoon olive oil

1 tablespoon chopped fresh tarragon

Pepper

1 cup chanterelle mushrooms, cleaned

1 cup Pickling Juice (see Appendices)

1 cup Sauternes

2 tablespoons butter

3/4 cup baked, peeled, and riced sweet potato

Salt

Foie Gras Custard (recipe follows)

2 tablespoons finely cut fresh chives

Foie Gras Ice Cream (recipe follows)

Cured Foie Gras (recipe follows)

Seared Foie Gras (recipe follows)

1 tablespoon fresh flat-leaf parsley chiffonade

Foie Gras Terrine (recipe follows)

Fleur de sel

METHOD To prepare the citrus salad: Cut the citrus sections into thirds and toss together in a bowl. Add the olive oil and tarragon and season with pepper.

To prepare the mushrooms: Thinly slice the mushrooms and place in a container with the Pickling Juice. Refrigerate for 2 hours. Drain the mushrooms just prior to serving.

To prepare the sweet potato purée: Place the Sauternes in a small saucepan and simmer over medium heat for 15 minutes, or until reduced to 1/2 cup. Add the butter and purée with the riced sweet potato. Place the purée in a small saucepan, warm over medium heat, and season to taste with salt and pepper.

ASSEMBLY Place a Foie Gras Custard in the upper right hand corner of each plate and sprinkle with the chives. Spoon some of the citrus salad just below the custard and place a "quenelle" of the Foie Gras Ice Cream alongside. Place a piece of the Cured Foie Gras on the bottom right-hand corner and spoon some of the pickled mushrooms over the foie gras. Spoon the sweet potato purée in the upper left-hand corner and top with a piece of the Seared Foie Gras. Sprinkle with the parsley. Place the julienned Buddha's hand and some of its cooking liquid on the bottom left-hand corner of the plate, top with a slice of the Foie Gras Terrine, and sprinkle with the fleur de sel.

Foie Gras Custard

Yield: 12 1/2-ounce custards

5 ounces foie gras, cleaned

3 eggs

1 cup heavy whipping cream

Salt and pepper

METHOD Preheat the oven to 300 degrees. Purée the foie gras, eggs, and cream in a food processor until smooth. Season with salt and pepper. Pour the mixture into twelve 1/2-ounce ramekins. Place the ramekins on a sheet pan and add warm water to the sheet pan to a depth of 1/4 inch. Bake for 20 minutes, or until slightly firm. Cool the custards slightly before serving.

Foie Gras Ice Cream

Yield: approximately 3 cups

1 shallot, minced

1 tablespoon foie gras fat

1 cup peeled, chopped Granny Smith apple

8 ounces foie gras, cleaned

2 cups Duck Stock (see Appendices)

4 sprigs tarragon

Salt and pepper

METHOD Sauté the shallot with the foie gras fat in a small sauté pan for 1 minute over medium heat. Add the apple and cook for 10 minutes, or until the apple is tender. Place the foie gras in a medium saucepan and add the Duck Stock and tarragon sprigs. Simmer over medium-low heat for 15 minutes, or until it reaches an internal temperature of 125 degrees. Discard the tarragon. Purée the foie gras with the Duck Stock and the apple mixture until smooth. Season to taste with salt and pepper and pour into a shallow pan. Freeze for 2 hours, or until solid.

Chop the frozen foie gras and purée in a food processor. Pour back into the shallow pan and freeze until firm.

Cured Foie Gras

Yield: 3 by 5-inch pan

10 ounces foie gras

1 teaspoon ground nutmeg

Salt and pepper

1/4 cup Sauternes

2 tablespoons sugar

3 cups sea salt

5 cups chanterelle mushrooms, cleaned

1 Spanish onion, chopped

6 sprigs thyme

1 bulb garlic, halved

1 quart water

6 sheets gelatin

METHOD Warm the foie gras to room temperature, cut open like a book, and remove any veins. Press the foie gras firmly with your fingers to soften it and season with nutmeg, salt, and pepper. Sprinkle with the Sauternes and sugar. Close the foie gras, returning it to its original shape, and wrap tightly in cheesecloth. Cover the bottom of a container with a layer of the sea salt and lay the foie gras over the salt. Cover the foie gras with the remaining sea salt and place an object of moderate weight over the foie gras. Refrigerate for 2 days.

Remove the salt from the foie gras and unwrap it from the cheesecloth. Line a 3 by 5 by ½-inch container with plastic wrap. Spread the foie gras into the container in a ½-inch-thick layer, smoothing the surface. Refrigerate for 1 hour, or until firm.

Place the mushrooms in a stockpot with the onion, thyme, and garlic. Cover with the water and simmer over medium-low heat for 1 hour. Strain through a fine-mesh sieve, discarding the solids. Cook the liquid over medium heat for 45 minutes, or until reduced to 2 cups. Bloom the gelatin in a bowl of cold water for 5 minutes. Remove the gelatin from the water and add it to the warm stock. Whisk the stock until the gelatin is incorporated and cool to room temperature. Pour a ¼-inch-thick layer of the chanterelle gelatin over the cured foie gras and refrigerate until set. Cut the cured foie gras into 12 pieces ½ by 1½ inches long.

Seared Foie Gras

Yield: 12 1-ounce pieces

2 ounces chopped bacon
1 tablespoon minced shallot
2 cups loosely packed finely shredded
purple cabbage
1 sprig rosemary
¼ cup red wine
¼ cup Port
⅓ cup chopped golden raisins
Salt and pepper
1 tablespoon chopped fresh flat-leaf parsley
12 1½-ounce portions foie gras, cleaned

METHOD Cook the bacon in a medium sauté pan over medium heat for 3 minutes, or until the fat is rendered. Add the shallot and cook for 1 minute. Add the cabbage and

rosemary and cook for 3 minutes. Add the red wine and Port and cook over low heat for 30 minutes, or until the cabbage is tender. Discard the rosemary and add the raisins. Cook for 2 minutes, season to taste with salt and pepper, and fold in the parsley.

Season the foie gras to taste with salt and pepper. Place in a hot sauté pan over medium heat and cook for 45 seconds on each side, or until just cooked. Place some of the cabbage mixture over the seared foie gras.

Foie Gras Terrine

Yield: 8 by 1½ by 2¼-inch terrine

1 Buddha's hand fruit
2 cups sugar
2 cups water
2 pounds foie gras, cleaned
Fleur de sel
White pepper
1 teaspoon five-spice powder
1 cup Armagnac
Salt and pepper

METHOD Cut off and discard the "fingers" from the Buddha's hand. Using a mandoline, thinly slice the remaining fruit ⅛ inch thick. Blanch the slices briefly in boiling water and drain. Repeat this process 4 times. Place 2 cups of the sugar and the water in a saucepan and bring to a simmer. Add the blanched slices and simmer over low heat for 15 minutes. Remove from the heat and let cool.

Work the foie gras with your fingers to soften it and season with the fleur de sel, white pepper, and five-spice powder. Roll the foie gras into an oval shape, wrap very tightly in plastic wrap, and refrigerate for 2 hours. Remove the plastic from the foie gras and place it and two-thirds of the candied Buddha's hand in a resealable freezer bag. (Reserve the remaining Buddha's hand and the cooking liquid for serving.) Pour the Armagnac over the foie gras, seal the bag, and refrigerate for 2 days. Place the foie gras bag in another resealable bag, place in a saucepan, and cover with cold

water. Bring the water to a slow simmer over medium-low heat and cook for 15 minutes, or until the foie gras reaches an internal temperature of 125 degrees. Drain the foie gras in a large-holed sieve, discarding the fat and cooking juices. Reserve the Buddha's hand and foie gras separately.

Line an 8 by 1½ by 2¼-inch terrine mold with plastic wrap, allowing some to drape over the sides. Spread a ½-inch-thick layer of the foie gras in the bottom of the mold and season with salt and pepper. Cut the Buddha's hand to fit the width of the mold and place an even layer of the Buddha's hand over the foie gras. Continue to layer the foie gras in ½-inch-thick layers, covering each layer with Buddha's hand, until there are 3 layers of Buddha's hand and 4 layers of foie gras. Fold the excess plastic wrap over the terrine and refrigerate for 3 hours, or until firm. Cut the reserved Buddha's hand into julienne and toss with the cooking liquid from the Buddha's hand.

Remove the terrine from the mold and rewrap tightly in plastic wrap. With the plastic wrap on, slice the terrine into ⅜-inch-thick slices. Carefully remove the plastic wrap and season with salt and pepper.

Substitutions

Chicken liver, squab liver, duck liver

Wine Notes

The classic pairing of Sauternes with foie gras holds true with this dish. The diversity of the 5 foie gras preparations offers an opportunity to explore many variations on that theme, however. While the sometimes almost-tropical Quarts de Chaume from Domaine des Baumard sings with the sweet candied Buddha's hand fruit in the terrine, and sweet St. Croix du Mont from Château La Rame cuts through the buttery custard, a well-balanced Bonnezeaux from Château de Fesles, with its lush texture and firm acidity, complements the entire presentation.

Hazelnut-Crusted Calf's Liver with Sweet-and-Sour Spinach, Apple-Quince Purée, and Mustard Jus

*In general, calf's liver can be pretty humble and unspectacular. But with the
addition of a few added flavor and texture notes, it can be elevated to something sublime.
Here, an apple-quince purée provides a complexly flavored sweet foil, yet a
Pommery mustard jus balances the sweetness and adds a sharp note to cut the richness of the liver.
A crust of meaty Ennis hazelnuts provides crunchy texture and a rich earthiness.
Wilted spinach accented with flavors of sweet and sour weaves everything together.*

Serves 4

12 ounces calf's liver, cleaned

3 cups milk

Salt and pepper

1/2 cup flour

1 egg, lightly beaten

*1/2 cup toasted, skinned, and chopped
Ennis hazelnuts*

1 tablespoon grapeseed oil

1 red apple, peeled and diced

1 quince, peeled and diced

7 tablespoons butter

1/4 cup water

*2 red apples, skin on, cored and cut into
1/2-inch-thick rings*

1 shallot, thinly sliced

3 ounces baby spinach

2 tablespoons brown sugar

1/4 cup apple cider vinegar

2 tablespoons Pommery mustard

*1/2 cup Veal Stock Reduction
(see Appendices)*

1 tablespoon fine diagonal–cut fresh chives

METHOD To prepare the liver: Soak the calf's liver in milk for 2 hours. Remove from the milk and cut into 3-ounce pieces. Season with salt and pepper and lightly dust with some of the flour. Coat the liver with the egg, then lightly dust with flour again, and coat with the hazelnuts. Sear the liver with the grapeseed oil in a hot sauté pan over medium-high heat for 2 minutes on each side, or until cooked medium-rare. Cut each piece into 4 slices.

To prepare the apple-quince purée: Sauté the diced apple and the quince in 2 tablespoons of the butter over medium-low heat for 8 to 10 minutes, or until tender. Purée with the water until smooth and pass through a fine-mesh sieve. Season to taste with salt and pepper.

To prepare the apples: Place the apple rings in a hot sauté pan with 3 tablespoons of the butter and cook over medium heat for 2 to 3 minutes on each side, or until lightly golden brown. Remove the apples from the pan and cut each ring into 4 pieces.

To prepare the spinach: Sweat the shallot in the remaining 2 tablespoons butter in a small sauté pan over medium heat for 3 minutes, or until translucent. Add the spinach and cook for 1 minute. Add the sugar and apple cider vinegar and cook for 3 minutes, or until most of the liquid has been absorbed. Season with salt and pepper.

To prepare the mustard jus: Whisk the mustard into the Veal Stock Reduction in a small saucepan and simmer over medium heat for 2 minutes.

ASSEMBLY Place some of the spinach in the center of each plate and top with 3 calf's liver slices. Spoon the apple-quince purée and the mustard jus around the liver. Place some of the apple pieces around the plate and sprinkle with the chives. Top with freshly ground black pepper.

Substitutions

Chicken liver, chicken, pork

Wine Notes

Here, the rich calf's liver is tempered by the sweet fruit purée, the crust of crunchy hazelnuts, and the delicate mustard jus. Sweet Chenin Blanc from the Loire Valley echoes the subtly caramelized fruit tones of the apple and quince. A lush style, such as Vouvray Moelleux, provides a mirror for the supple textures, and its botrytised character makes it an interesting companion for the nuts. The best producers, such as Domaine Gaston Huet, balance the unctuousness of their wine with a good dose of fruity acidity. Try Huet's Vouvray *Le Mont* or *Clos de Bourg Moelleux*.

Bleeding Heart Radish Terrine with Star Anise and Thyme-Flavored Foie Gras and Seckel Pear

This is a delightful combination of flavors and textures. Foie gras,
seared and flavored with star anise and thyme leaves, rests on a julienne of Seckel pear.
Adjacent to it is a slice of radish terrine that is a perfect textural and flavor contrast
to the liver. The radish has a natural sweetness and just enough playful bite to offset the fois gras.
Finally, the crispy pear "chip" adds both a whimsical touch and a delicate sweetness.

Serves 12

8 large bleeding heart radishes

¼ cup olive oil

4 bay leaves

1 cup plus 3 tablespoons white wine vinegar

12 sprigs thyme

5 sheets gelatin

2 cups Vegetable Stock (see Appendices)

¼ cup loosely packed chopped fresh chives

Salt and pepper

¼ cup sugar

1 tablespoon water

12 2-ounce pieces foie gras, cleaned

2 star anise, finely ground

4 teaspoons fresh thyme leaves

2 cups julienned Seckel pear, skin on

1 cup Veal Stock Reduction, hot (see Appendices)

3 tablespoons Basil Oil (see Appendices)

12 Oven-Dried Pear Chips (see Appendices)

METHOD To prepare the terrine: Double bag 4 resealable plastic freezer bags and place 2 bleeding heart radishes, 1 tablespoon olive oil, 1 bay leaf, ¼ cup of the white wine vinegar, and 3 thyme sprigs in each bag. Seal the bags and place in a large saucepan of simmering water. Cook for 45 minutes to 1 hour, or until tender. Cool in the bags, peel, and trim the radishes to the width of the terrine mold, reserving the scraps. Slice the radishes ⅛ inch thick.

Bloom the gelatin in a bowl of cold water for 5 minutes. Remove the gelatin from the water and place in a saucepan with the Vegetable Stock. Warm the stock over medium-low heat (do not allow to boil) for 2 minutes, or until the gelatin is dissolved, and add the chives.

Line an 8 by 1½ by 2¼-inch terrine mold with plastic wrap allowing some to drape over the sides. Dip the radish slices into the gelatin mixture and place in an even layer on the bottom of the terrine mold. Season with salt and pepper and continue to layer the radish slices until the terrine is full. Firmly press down on the terrine with your fingers or a small wooden board. Fold the excess plastic wrap over the terrine and refrigerate for 3 hours, or until firm.

Preheat the oven to 450 degrees. Remove the terrine from the mold and rewrap tightly in plastic wrap. Cut the terrine into 12 ½-inch-thick slices and lay on a sheet pan. Carefully remove the plastic wrap and season with salt and pepper. Flash in the oven for 2 minutes just prior to serving.

To prepare the radish juice: Place the sugar and water in a small sauté pan and cook over medium heat for 5 to 7 minutes, or until caramelized. Add the remaining 3 tablespoons white wine vinegar and the reserved radish pieces and cook for 7 minutes. Strain, discarding the radish pieces, and set the liquid aside.

To prepare the foie gras: Season the foie gras with salt and pepper. Place in a hot sauté pan and cook over medium-high heat for 2 minutes on each side, or until just cooked. Remove the foie gras from the pan and sprinkle with the star anise and some of the thyme leaves. Place the pear in the pan with the foie gras fat and cook for 3 minutes, or until just warm. Drain off any fat and reserve. Season with salt and pepper.

ASSEMBLY Place some of the pear left of center on each plate and top with a piece of foie gras. Place a slice of the terrine next to the pear. Spoon the Veal Stock Reduction, Basil Oil, radish juice, and reserved foie gras fat around the plate. Sprinkle the thyme leaves around the plate and insert a pear chip between the foie gras and terrine.

Substitutions

Chicken liver, chicken, pork, scallops

Wine Notes

With its earthy feel, the sweet Monbazillac from Château Tirecul la Gravière can put the focus on the seared foie gras element, while also resounding with the character of the bleeding heart radishes. The whole dish is taken into red wine territory, however, by the prominent thyme notes and Veal Stock Reduction. A rich style of Vosne-Romanée, such as *Les Brûlées* from Leroy, lends the excitement of heady perfumes and sumptuous textures of Pinot Noir to the whole.

Rabbit Loin with Chanterelle Mushrooms and Sundried Tomato "Tart"

This light, free-form tart is both refreshing and deeply satisfying. The sundried tomato
pieces and baby spinach provide cleansing and piquant notes, while the chanterelle mushrooms and
the Vidalia onion purée add earthiness. The rabbit loin is just meaty enough to stand
up to the other flavors. Foie gras pieces could be added if a richer result were desired, or a red wine
reduction could be drizzled around the finished dish if a luscious red wine were on the menu.

Serves 4

1 cup finely chopped chanterelle mushrooms

1¼ cups butter

Salt and pepper

¼ cup finely chopped oil-packed sundried tomatoes, oil blotted off

2 cups flour, plus additional for dusting

1 teaspoon salt

1 egg yolk

⅓ cup plus ½ cup water

1 Vidalia onion, julienned

1½ cups whole chanterelle mushrooms, cleaned

4 rabbit tenderloins

2 tablespoons grapeseed oil

4 rabbit kidneys

2 cups loosely packed baby spinach

4 oil-packed sundried tomatoes, quartered

8 cloves Roasted Garlic (see Appendices)

½ cup Meat Stock Reduction, hot (see Appendices)

4 teaspoons olive oil

4 teaspoons micro arugula sprouts

METHOD To prepare the tart base: Cook the chopped mushrooms with 1 tablespoon of the butter in a small sauté pan over low heat, stirring occasionally, for 20 to 30 minutes, or until dry. Season to taste with salt and pepper and cool to room temperature. Toss the mushrooms and chopped sundried tomatoes in a small bowl and set aside.

Preheat the oven to 350 degrees. Mix the flour, 1 teaspoon salt, 1 cup of the butter, and the mushroom mixture in the bowl of an electric mixer and beat on low speed until the ingredients are combined and the butter is in pea-sized chunks. Add the egg yolk and ⅓ cup of water all at once and mix until the dough just begins to come together. Remove the dough to a lightly floured work surface and form it into a ball. Cover the dough in plastic wrap and refrigerate for at least 30 minutes. Roll the dough out on a lightly floured surface ⅛ inch thick and cut into four 6 by 2-inch pieces. Place the dough pieces on a parchment-lined sheet pan and bake for 15 minutes, or until golden brown. Extra dough may be frozen.

To prepare the onion purée: Cook the onion with 2 tablespoons of the butter in a small sauté pan over medium heat for 10 minutes, or until golden brown. Add the remaining ½ cup water and cook for 1 minute. Purée until smooth and season to taste with salt and pepper. Warm the purée in a small saucepan just prior to serving.

To prepare the mushrooms: Cut the whole chanterelle mushrooms in half and place in a hot sauté pan with the remaining 1 tablespoon butter. Cook over medium heat for 5 minutes, or until tender. Season to taste with salt and pepper.

To prepare the rabbit: Season the rabbit tenderloins with salt and pepper. Place the tenderloins in a hot sauté pan with the grapeseed oil and cook over medium-high heat for 3 minutes on each side, or until slightly undercooked. Remove the tenderloins from the pan and set aside. Add the kidneys to the pan and cook for 1 minute on each side. Season to taste with salt and pepper and remove the kidneys from the pan. Quickly toss the spinach and the quartered sundried tomatoes in the pan and cook for 1 minute, or until warm. Season the spinach mixture to taste with salt and pepper. Cut the rabbit tenderloins into ½-inch-thick slices on the diagonal and season to taste with salt and pepper.

ASSEMBLY Smear 2 of the Roasted Garlic cloves on each tart base and place in the center of each plate. Arrange the rabbit loins, mushrooms, and spinach mixture over the tart bases. Place a kidney at the front of each tart and spoon the onion purée and Meat Stock Reduction around the tart. Drizzle the olive oil around the plate and sprinkle with the arugula sprouts.

Substitutions

Duck, chicken, scallops

Wine Notes

The crunchy tomato-cracker base provides an interesting textural contrast for the smooth caramelized onion purée and rabbit. Roasted Garlic adds additional sweetness, and the chanterelles bring a fruity note. A Barbera from Piedmont that does not take itself too seriously is a lively match for this dish. With youthful fruit and soft tannins, Barbera d'Asti *Pomorosso* from Coppo is an ideal selection.

Smoked Veal Sweetbreads with Fingerling Potatoes, Cinnamon Cap Mushroom Broth, and Rosemary

Infusing sweetbreads, an already delicious and elegant meat, creates an extraordinary dish. Slices of fingerling potatoes contribute substance, and delicate cinnamon cap mushrooms introduce just the right earthiness. Everything swims in a clean, light mushroom broth that creates a harmonious backdrop for the other elements. Notes of rosemary provide freshness.

Serves 4

4 3-ounce veal sweetbreads

2 cups chopped Spanish onion

1 cup chopped leek

1½ cups chopped celery root

9 sprigs rosemary

3 cups hickory wood chips, soaked in water for 1 hour

Salt and pepper

2 tablespoons grapeseed oil

3 shallots, minced

½ cup butter

3 cups cinnamon cap mushrooms, cleaned

8 cups Mushroom Stock (see Appendices)

1 teaspoon apple cider vinegar

8 fingerling potatoes, baked and sliced ¼ inch thick

8 purple fingerling potatoes, baked and sliced ¼ inch thick

METHOD To prepare the sweetbreads: Rinse the sweetbreads in cold water. Place the onion, leek, celery root, and 3 of the rosemary sprigs in a large saucepan. Add the sweetbreads and cover with cold water. Bring to a simmer over medium heat and simmer for 3 minutes. Remove from the heat and let sit for 15 minutes.

Remove the sweetbreads from the liquid and pat dry. Place the sweetbreads and 3 of the rosemary sprigs in a smoker or covered grill with the hickory chips and smoke over medium-low heat for 30 minutes. Remove from the smoker and season to taste with salt and pepper. Place the sweetbreads in a hot sauté pan with the grapeseed oil and sear over medium-high heat for 2 to 3 minutes on each side, or until golden brown. Add 1 rosemary sprig and cook for 30 seconds. Remove the sweetbreads from the pan and slice in half on a very severe diagonal.

To prepare the mushrooms: Sweat the shallots in 2 tablespoons of the butter in a large saucepan over medium heat for 2 to 3 minutes, or until translucent. Add the mushrooms and cook for 5 to 7 minutes, or until tender. Add the Mushroom Stock and simmer over medium-low heat for 30 minutes. Add 1 rosemary sprig and the apple cider vinegar and simmer for 2 minutes. Whisk in the remaining 6 tablespoons butter and add the fingerling potatoes. Season to taste with salt and pepper.

ASSEMBLY Ladle some of the mushroom broth into each shallow bowl. Place 2 halves of the sweetbreads and some of the leaves from the remaining rosemary sprig in the center of each bowl. Top with freshly ground black pepper.

Substitutions

Chicken, veal, pork

Wine Notes

The smoky flavors and herbal components in this dish lead one to the red wines of the southern Rhône Valley and Provence, particularly, muscular, *garrigue*-scented Gigondas from Domaine Les Paillieres. A blend of predominantly Grenache, Syrah, Cinsault, and Mourvèdre, it has a smoked meatiness wrapped around a core of dark berry fruit that plays with the almost-fruity cinnamon cap mushrooms and intense sweetbreads.

Duck Liver with Candied Turnips and Portobello Mushroom Vinaigrette

Duck livers with just a little help can become a stunning preparation. They are paired here with luscious candied turnips, which in turn are offset with tart cranberry pieces. An earthy portobello mushroom vinaigrette provides just the right canvas for these sensual but muscular flavors to shine.

Serves 4

4 portobello mushrooms, cleaned and stems removed

2 1/2 cups water

3 sprigs thyme

1/2 cup olive oil

Salt and pepper

1 1/2 tablespoons chopped fresh chives

1 1/2 tablespoons sherry wine vinegar

16 baby turnips, peeled and stems trimmed to 1/4 inch

2 cups milk

1/2 cup plus 2 tablespoons sugar

1/4 cup butter

2 cups cranberries

4 duck livers, cleaned

2 tablespoons grapeseed oil

4 teaspoons fresh tiny sage leaves

METHOD To prepare the mushrooms: Preheat the oven to 375 degrees. Place the portobello mushrooms, 1 cup of the water, the thyme, and 1 tablespoon of the olive oil in a small roasting pan. Season with salt and pepper and cover with aluminum foil. Roast in the oven for 30 minutes, or until tender. Cool the mushrooms to room temperature. Transfer the cooking juices to a small saucepan and cook over low heat for 30 minutes, or until reduced to 1/4 cup.

Reserve the reduced liquid for the vinaigrette. Remove the gills from the mushrooms, cut 3 of the mushrooms into large dice, and warm just prior to serving. Cut the remaining mushroom into a brunoise.

To prepare the vinaigrette: Whisk together the portobello brunoise, reserved mushroom cooking liquid, chives, the remaining 7 tablespoons olive oil, and the sherry wine vinegar in a small bowl and season to taste with salt and pepper.

To prepare the turnips: Place the turnips, milk, 1/2 cup of the sugar, and 1 cup of the water in a medium saucepan over medium heat and cook for 10 to 15 minutes, or until tender. Remove the turnips, discarding the liquid. Just prior to serving, cook the turnips in the butter and the remaining 2 tablespoons sugar in a small sauté pan over medium heat for 2 to 3 minutes, or until golden brown and candied. Season to taste with salt and pepper.

To prepare the cranberries: Cut the cranberries into quarters and place in a saucepan with the remaining 1/2 cup water. Slowly simmer the cranberries over low heat for 10 minutes, or until tender.

To prepare the livers: Season the duck livers with salt and pepper. Place the livers in a hot sauté pan with the grapeseed oil and cook over medium heat for 2 minutes on each side, or until cooked medium. Remove from the pan and let rest for 1 minute. Slice each liver in half and season to taste with salt and pepper.

ASSEMBLY Place some of the cranberries in the center of each plate and around the perimeter. Place 2 slices of the duck liver on top of the cranberries. Arrange 4 candied turnips and some of the large-diced mushroom around the plate. Spoon the portobello vinaigrette around the plate. Sprinkle with the sage leaves and top with freshly ground black pepper.

Substitutions

Foie gras, turkey, scallops

Wine Notes

The richly flavored duck liver contrasts with the sweet turnips and cranberries, while the mushroom vinaigrette and the herbs tie everything together. The earthy richness of Côtes de Provence reds, such as the *Cuvée Speciale* from Domaine de Grandpère, and Bandol reds, such as those from Château Pradeaux, are a particularly good complement for the portobello and for the prominent sage and thyme.

Cubed Beef and Barley Stew with Button Porcini Mushrooms, Foie Gras Beignet, and Thyme

~~~~~~

This twist on a beef and barley stew features some extravagant touches. First, rather than being cooked to the point of blandness and chewiness, the beef is left medium-rare in order to showcase its flavor and succulence. Button porcini mushrooms add an elegant earthiness, and notes of thyme provide the perfect distinctive flavor enhancement. The pièce de résistance, however, is a beignet concealing a cube of foie gras. This element provides a richness and luxury that elevates the entire dish to another level. The dish could easily be served as a meal in itself.

Serves 4

12 green brussels sprouts, quartered

12 tiny purple brussels sprouts

3 tablespoons butter

Salt and pepper

1 4-ounce beef tenderloin

4 teaspoons grapeseed oil

2 cups cooked pearl barley, hot

8 baby carrots, parboiled and sliced into thin disks

2 stalks celery, cut into small dice

12 button porcini mushrooms, cleaned, parboiled, and halved

8 purple pearl onions, parboiled

8 cups Beef Consommé, hot (see Appendices)

4 teaspoons fresh thyme leaves

Foie Gras Beignet (recipe follows)

4 teaspoons foie gras fat

METHOD To prepare the brussels sprouts: Place the green and purple brussels sprouts in a hot sauté pan with the butter and cook over medium heat, turning occasionally, for 5 to 6 minutes, or until caramelized. Season to taste with salt and pepper.

To prepare the beef: Season the beef with salt and pepper. Place the beef in a hot sauté pan with the grapeseed oil and cook over medium-high heat for 4 minutes on each side, or until cooked medium-rare. Remove the meat from pan and let rest for 3 minutes. Cut the beef into ¼-inch dice and season to taste with salt and pepper.

ASSEMBLY Arrange some of the barley, carrots, celery, mushrooms, brussels sprouts, pearl onions, and beef in each bowl. Ladle in some of the hot Beef Consommé and sprinkle with the thyme leaves. Slice each Foie Gras Beignet in half and place in the center of the stew. Drizzle some of the foie gras fat around the bowl and top with freshly ground black pepper.

Foie Gras Beignet

Yield: 4 beignets

½ cup lukewarm water

Pinch of active dry yeast

½ teaspoon sugar

¾ cup plus 3½ tablespoons flour

Pinch of salt

3 ounces foie gras, cleaned and cut into ½-inch-thick slices

1 egg, lightly beaten

METHOD Combine the lukewarm water, yeast, and sugar in a small bowl. Let stand for 15 minutes, or until frothy. Sift together the flour and salt into a medium bowl, add the yeast mixture, and stir until a dough forms. Turn out onto a floured surface and knead for 10 minutes, or until the dough is smooth and elastic. Transfer to a small oiled bowl, cover, and let rise for 1 hour.

Place the foie gras in the freezer for at least 30 minutes, or until completely frozen.

Preheat the oven to 375 degrees. Punch down the dough and divide into 4 equal portions. Roll out each portion into a ⅛-inch-thick circle and top with a piece of the frozen fois gras. Fold over the dough to form a half-moon shape and pinch the edges to seal tightly. Brush lightly with the egg and bake for 12 minutes, or until golden brown. Serve hot.

Substitutions

Veal, chicken, lamb

Wine Notes

This rich, hearty, cold-weather dish, made even more luxurious by the buttery pastry-wrapped foie gras, points to a classically styled red wine. Tempranillo from Rioja easily handles the vegetable elements of celery and brussels sprouts. An aged wine like a *Gran Reserva* Rioja from Montecillo drapes the stew with ripe fruit and brown spices and keeps the diner warm.

Veal Sweetbreads with Medjool Dates, Crosnes, Black Truffles, Potato Purée, and Veal Stock Reduction

This dish is extremely sensual and heady, and although the individual ingredients are relatively simple and straightforward, the whole is decidedly greater than the sum of its parts. As one digs down through the Potato Purée, the surprises and aromas begin. The most intense, of course, is the black truffle, but it is the diverse textures and flavors of the sweetbreads, crosnes, and dates that make this preparation sing. A Veal Stock Reduction drizzled along the top of the purée adds a distinctive note of richness. This is the kind of dish that prompts a hush to fall over the dinner table the moment it is served.

Serves 4

1 tablespoon minced shallot

2 tablespoons butter

1/2 cup finely julienned black truffle

2 tablespoons brandy

2 tablespoons Madeira

2/3 cup Veal Stock Reduction, hot (see Appendices)

Salt and pepper

4 Braised Veal Sweetbreads nuggets (see Appendices)

16 crosnes, parboiled

2 Medjool dates, pitted, peeled, and cut into sixths

1 large black truffle, thinly sliced

3 cups warm Potato Purée (see Appendices)

2 teaspoons olive oil

16 fresh chervil leaves

Fleur de sel

METHOD To prepare the truffle purée: Cook the shallot in 1 tablespoon of the butter in a small saucepan over medium heat for 1 minute. Add 1/4 cup of the julienned truffles and cook for 1 minute. Add the brandy and Madeira to deglaze the pan, then cook for 1 to 2 minutes, or until thick and syrupy. Purée the truffles with just enough Veal Stock Reduction to create a paste. Season to taste with salt and pepper.

To prepare the sweetbreads: Cook the sweetbreads with the remaining 1 tablespoon butter in a small sauté pan over medium heat for 5 minutes, or until golden brown and crispy.

ASSEMBLY Spoon some of the truffle purée in the center of each cone-shaped bowl and sprinkle with the remaining julienned truffles. Cut the sweetbread nuggets in half and arrange them in the bowl along with the crosnes and dates. Top with freshly ground black pepper. Arrange the truffle slices over the mixture, completely covering it. Spoon the potato purée over the truffle slices, completely covering the truffles. Spoon the remaining Veal Stock Reduction around the outside ring of the bowl. Drizzle the olive oil over the center of the purée and arrange 4 chervil leaves in the center of the bowl. Sprinkle the fleur de sel on the purée.

Substitutions

Chicken, wild mushrooms, scallops

Wine Notes

Full-bodied, oak-aged Sangiovese is a vibrant foil for the high-density elements in this dish. Creamy veal sweetbreads and rich potatoes are complemented by a mature red from Tuscany such as Castellare's I *Sodi San Niccolo* from a ripe vintage.

Duck Breast with Sausage of Pig's Foot, Foie Gras, and Lobster with Red Wine–Shellfish Emulsion

After the duck breast has been cooked and sliced and the pieces placed on the plate,
it is enhanced with elements that are both humble and extravagant. Leek and chicken mushrooms add
the ideal textural notes. The transcendent element, though, is the sausage of pig's foot, lobster,
and foie gras, as it provides an almost decadent burst of flavor and mouthfeel. (Sheep casing is far more delicate
than pig casing, making it preferred here with these rather delicate elements.) Shellfish Oil and a
Red Wine–Shellfish Emulsion help to drive home the lobster flavor.

Serves 4

4 ounces foie gras, cleaned

Salt and pepper

¼ cup chopped Crispy Pig's Foot
(see Appendices)

1 lobster tail, cooked and small diced

1 teaspoon fresh thyme leaves

1 tablespoon chopped fresh flat-leaf parsley

20 inches sheep casing, rinsed

2½ cups chicken mushrooms

1 tablespoon minced shallot

2 tablespoons butter

1½ cups Chicken Stock (see Appendices)

1 teaspoon rice vinegar

4 tiny leeks, cleaned

2 medium duck breasts, skin scored and
excess fat trimmed

Red Wine–Shellfish Emulsion
(see Appendices)

8 teaspoons Shellfish Oil (see Appendices)

2 teaspoons fresh rosemary leaves

METHOD To prepare the sausage: Season the foie gras with salt and pepper. Place in a hot sauté pan and cook over medium heat for 2 minutes on each side. Cool the foie gras to room temperature and cut into small dice. Toss together the foie gras, Crispy Pig's Foot, lobster, thyme, and parsley in a medium bowl and season to taste with salt and pepper.

Preheat the oven to 400 degrees. Place the sausage mixture in a pastry bag fitted with a ½-inch round tip. Tie a knot at one end of the casing and place the other end over the pastry tip. Holding the casing on the pastry tip, slowly pipe the filling into the casing, packing it tightly. Once the casing is full of the mixture, twist it into 2½-inch-long sausages and tie a knot at the open end. Place the sausages on a roasting pan and roast for 10 to 12 minutes, or until golden brown. Slice each sausage in half on the diagonal.

To prepare the mushrooms: Sauté the mushrooms with the shallot and butter in a medium sauté pan over medium heat for 2 minutes. Add ½ cup of the Chicken Stock and the vinegar and cook for 3 to 5 minutes, or until the mushrooms are tender. Season to taste with salt and pepper. (Reserve the cooking juices from the mushrooms.) Purée one-third of the mushrooms with ½ cup of the Chicken Stock. Warm the mushroom purée just prior to serving.

To prepare the leeks: Place the leeks in a sauté pan with the remaining ½ cup Chicken Stock. Cover and simmer over medium heat for 15 minutes, or until tender. Remove the leeks from the stock, slice into 1½-inch pieces on the diagonal, and season to taste with salt and pepper.

To prepare the duck: Season the duck breasts with salt and pepper. Place them, skin side down, in a hot sauté pan and cook over medium heat for 6 to 7 minutes on each side, or until cooked medium. Let rest for 3 minutes and thinly slice. Season to taste with salt and pepper.

ASSEMBLY Place some of the sautéed mushrooms, 2 slices of sausage, and 3 pieces of the leeks on each plate. Arrange the sliced duck meat over the mushrooms. Spoon the mushroom purée and reserved mushrooms juices around the plate. Spoon the Red Wine–Shellfish Emulsion over the duck and around the plate. Drizzle the Shellfish Oil around the plate and sprinkle with the rosemary leaves. Top with freshly ground black pepper.

Substitutions

Squab, beef, veal

Wine Notes

The rich sausage and duck meat call for a full-bodied red, and a powerful Syrah is tempting. Choose one with power and finesse such as Côte Rotie *Côte Blonde* from Rene Rostaing with smoky black fruit and serious persistence. Another interesting option is Andrew Murray's *Roasted Slope* Syrah from Santa Barbara, which emulates the northern Rhône style of Syrah with the ripe fruit of California.

Appendices

Basic Recipes

Oils

Basil Oil

Yield: 1½ cups

½ cup firmly packed fresh basil leaves
½ cup firmly packed spinach
¼ cup firmly packed fresh flat-leaf
parsley leaves
¼ cup olive oil
1 cup canola oil

METHOD Blanch the basil, spinach, and parsley in boiling salted water for 45 seconds. Immediately shock in ice water and drain. Coarsely chop the mixture and squeeze out the excess water. Purée with the olive and canola oils for 3 to 4 minutes, or until bright green. Pour into a container, cover, and refrigerate for 1 day.

Strain the oil through a fine-mesh sieve and discard the solids. Refrigerate for 1 day, decant, and refrigerate until ready to use or for up to 1 week.

Herb Oil

Yield: ½ cup

¼ cup firmly packed chopped fresh chives
¼ cup firmly packed fresh flat-leaf
parsley leaves
¼ cup firmly packed watercress leaves
½ cup grapeseed oil
¼ cup olive oil

Place the chives, parsley, and watercress with 1 tablespoon of the grapeseed oil in a small sauté pan and sauté over medium heat for 2 minutes, or until wilted. Immediately shock in ice water and drain. Coarsely chop the mixture and squeeze out the excess water. Purée with the remaining 7 tablespoons grapeseed oil and the olive oil for 3 to 4 minutes, or until bright green. Pour into a container, cover, and refrigerate for 1 day.

Strain the oil through a fine-mesh sieve and discard the solids. Refrigerate for 1 day, decant, and refrigerate until ready to use or for up to 2 weeks.

Rosemary Oil

Yield: ½ cup

½ cup firmly packed fresh rosemary leaves
1 cup firmly packed spinach
½ cup plus 1 tablespoon grapeseed oil
¼ cup olive oil

METHOD Sauté the rosemary and spinach with 1 tablespoon of the grapeseed oil in a small sauté pan over medium heat for 2 minutes, or until wilted. Immediately shock in ice water and drain. Coarsely chop the mixture and squeeze out the excess water. Purée with the remaining 7 tablespoons grapeseed oil and the olive oil for 3 to 4 minutes, or until bright green. Pour into a container, cover, and refrigerate for 1 day.

Strain the oil through a fine-mesh sieve and discard the solids. Refrigerate for 1 day, decant, and refrigerate until ready to use or for up to 2 weeks.

Shellfish Oil

Yield: ¾ cup

4 lobster heads
1 teaspoon tomato paste
1 cup canola oil

METHOD Preheat the oven to 400 degrees. Place the lobster heads in a roasting pan and roast for 40 minutes, or until they are bright red. Break up the heads and place in a small saucepan with the tomato paste and canola oil. Heat the mixture for 10 minutes, cool, and refrigerate for 2 days.

Strain the oil through a fine-mesh sieve lined with cheesecloth and discard the solids. Refrigerate until ready to use or for up to 2 weeks.

Braised Meats

Braised Beef Cheeks

Yield: 2 pounds

2 pounds beef cheeks
Salt and pepper
2 tablespoons grapeseed oil
2 cups chopped Spanish onion
1 cup chopped carrot
1 cup chopped celery
1 bulb garlic, peeled
2 cups red wine
2½ quarts Beef Stock (see page 228)
6 leaves fresh sage

METHOD To prepare the beef cheeks: Preheat the oven to 225 degrees. Season the beef cheeks with salt and pepper. Sear the beef cheeks in the grapeseed oil in a hot braising pan over medium-high heat for 2 minutes on each side, or until golden brown. Remove the beef cheeks and add the onion, carrot, celery, and garlic. Cook the vegetables for 3 to 4 minutes, or until golden brown and caramelized. Deglaze with the red wine and return the beef cheeks to the pan. Add the Beef Stock and bring the mixture to a slow simmer. Cover and braise in the oven for 4 hours, rotating the beef cheeks occasionally.

When the beef cheeks are extremely tender, remove from the liquid. Using a fork, pull the meat from the beef cheeks, finely shredding it. Season the meat with salt and pepper. Strain the liquid and place in a saucepan. Reduce the braising liquid over medium heat, skimming occasionally, until it reaches a saucelike consistency. Add the sage leaves, simmer for 3 minutes, and remove the sage leaves.

Braised Black Pig Shoulder

Yield: 1 pound

1 1¼-pound black pig shoulder, bones and sinew removed
Salt and pepper
2 tablespoons grapeseed oil
2 large Spanish onions, chopped
2 carrots, chopped
2 stalks celery, chopped
1 tomato, seeded and coarsely chopped
6 cloves garlic, chopped
½ cup chopped fresh ginger
(for ginger-braised)
1 cup red wine
4 cups Chicken Stock (see page 227)
1 bay leaf
6 sprigs thyme

METHOD To braise the black pig: Preheat the oven to 300 degrees. Season the black pig shoulder with salt and pepper. Divide the black pig into 4 equal portions and roll and tie up with butcher's twine. Cook the black pig with the grapeseed oil in a small roasting pan on the stovetop over medium-high heat for 3 minutes on each side, or until golden brown. Remove the black pig and set aside. Add the onions, carrots, celery, and tomato and cook for 7 to 10 minutes, or until golden brown and caramelized. Return the black pig to the pan and add the garlic, ginger (if using), red wine, Chicken Stock, bay leaf, and thyme. Season with salt and pepper, cover tightly, and braise in the oven for 4 to 5 hours, or until the meat is very tender.

If desired, strain the braising liquid, reduce it over medium heat until it reaches a saucelike consistency, and use it in place of Meat Stock Reduction.

Braised Lamb Shank

Yield: 3 lamb shanks

3 lamb shanks
Salt and pepper
1½ tablespoons olive oil
1 Spanish onion, coarsely chopped
1 carrot, coarsely chopped
1 stalk celery, coarsely chopped
1 bulb garlic, peeled and coarsely chopped
1 cup red wine
2 quarts Lamb Stock (see page 227)

METHOD Preheat the oven to 250 degrees. Season the shanks with salt and pepper. Sear the shanks with the olive oil in a large roasting pan over medium-high heat for 10 minutes, or until browned on all sides. Remove the shanks and set aside. Add the onion, carrot, celery, and garlic to the pan and cook for 10 minutes, or until golden brown. Deglaze with the red wine and return the lamb shanks to the pan. Add the Lamb Stock, cover tightly, and braise in the oven for 6 to 8 hours, or until the meat is very tender. Remove the lamb shanks from the pan and reserve the braising liquid.

Strain the braising liquid through a fine-mesh sieve and cook over medium-low heat for 30 minutes, or until reduced to 1 cup.

Braised Oxtail

Yield: approximately 2 cups

8 oxtails
2 tablespoons canola oil
1 large Spanish onion, chopped
1 carrot, chopped
1 stalk celery, chopped
4 cloves garlic, chopped
1 tomato, seeded and coarsely chopped
1 cup red wine
3 cups Chicken Stock (see below)
1 bay leaf
2 sprigs thyme
Salt and pepper

METHOD Preheat the oven to 325 degrees. Cook the oxtails with the canola oil in a small roasting pan on the stovetop over medium-high heat for 3 minutes on each side, or until golden brown. Remove the oxtails and set aside. Add the onion, carrot, celery, garlic, and tomato and cook for 7 to 10 minutes, or until golden brown and caramelized. Return the oxtails to the pan and add the red wine, Chicken Stock, bay leaf, and thyme. Season with salt and pepper, cover tightly, and cook in the oven for 3 hours, or until the meat is very tender. Remove the meat from the bones and discard the bones.

If desired, strain the braising liquid through a fine-mesh sieve, cook over medium-low heat for 30 minutes, or until reduced to 1 cup, and use as a sauce.

Braised Sweetbreads

Yield: 4 sweetbread nuggets

4 2- to 3-ounce sweetbread noisettes
1 cup chopped Spanish onion
1 cup chopped carrot
1 cup chopped celery
½ cup chopped leek
2 tablespoons grapeseed oil
3 sprigs thyme
3 cups Chicken Stock (see below)
Salt and pepper

METHOD Soak the sweetbreads in salted water overnight in the refrigerator. Remove from the refrigerator and run under cold water for 5 minutes.

Cook the onion, carrot, celery, and leek with the grapeseed oil in a medium saucepan over medium-high heat for 10 minutes, or until caramelized. Add the sweetbreads and thyme and cover with the Chicken Stock. Simmer the liquid, gently poaching the sweetbreads for 7 to 8 minutes, or until tender. Remove from the liquid, clean off any membranes or veins, and lightly season with salt and pepper.

Stocks and Reductions

Chicken Stock

Yield: 2 quarts

6 pounds chicken bones
3 cups chopped Spanish onion
2 cups chopped carrot
2 cups chopped celery
1 cup chopped leek
1 tablespoon white peppercorns
1 bay leaf

METHOD Place all of the ingredients in a large stockpot and add cold water to cover by three-quarters. Bring to a boil, reduce the heat to low, and simmer slowly, uncovered, for 4 hours, skimming every 30 minutes to remove impurities that rise to the surface. Strain through a fine-mesh sieve, discard the solids, and cook, uncovered, over medium heat for 30 to 45 minutes, or until reduced to 2 quarts. Store in the refrigerator for up to 4 days or freeze for up to 2 months.

Consommé

This recipe can be used to make any type of consommé, including chicken, beef, partridge, or pheasant.

Yield: 1½ quarts

2 quarts stock (such as chicken, beef, partridge, or pheasant)
6 egg whites
½ cup small-diced Spanish onion
⅓ cup small-diced carrot
⅓ cup small-diced celery
¼ cup small-diced tomato
1 pound ground meat (same type as the stock)
Salt and pepper

METHOD Place the stock in a large saucepan and cook over medium heat for 10 minutes, or until warm. Whisk together the egg whites, onion, carrot, celery, and tomato in a medium bowl until slightly frothy. Whisk in the ground meat. Whisk the egg mixture into the stock. Stir constantly in one motion with a wooden spoon for about 10 minutes, or until a raft begins to form. Stop stirring and reduce to a slow simmer. After the raft forms, break a small hole in the raft and continue to simmer for 45 minutes, or until the liquid appears crystal clear. Strain through a fine-mesh sieve lined with cheesecloth, being careful not to break the raft. Discard the raft and season the consommé to taste with salt and pepper.

Game Bird Stock

This recipe can be used to make any type of stock, including duck, grouse, partridge, pheasant, or squab.

Yield: approximately 1 quart

3 pounds bones (such as duck, grouse, partridge, pheasant, or squab)

1 cup chopped carrot

1 cup chopped celery

1 cup chopped Spanish onion

3 cloves garlic

2 tablespoons canola oil

1/2 cup chopped tomato

2 cups red wine

1 bay leaf

1 tablespoon peppercorns

METHOD Preheat the oven to 450 degrees. Place the bones in a roasting pan and roast for 30 to 45 minutes, or until golden brown. Turn the bones after 20 minutes to ensure even browning.

Place the carrot, celery, onion, and garlic with the canola oil in a large stockpot and sauté over high heat for 7 minutes, or until caramelized. Add the tomato and cook for 2 minutes. Deglaze the pan with the red wine and cook until most of the wine has been absorbed. Add the browned bones, bay leaf, and peppercorns and cover with cold water. Bring to a boil, reduce the heat to low, and simmer slowly, uncovered, for 4 hours, skimming every 30 minutes to remove impurities that rise to the surface. Strain through a fine-mesh sieve. Store in the refrigerator for up to 4 days or freeze for up to 2 months.

Game Bird Stock Reduction

This recipe can be used to make any type of reduction, including duck, grouse, partridge, pheasant, or squab.

Yield: 1 cup

1 Spanish onion, chopped

1 carrot, chopped

1 stalk celery, chopped

1 tablespoon grapeseed oil

1 small tomato, seeded and chopped

1/2 cup red wine

1 quart Game Bird Stock (such as duck, grouse, partridge, pheasant, or squab)

METHOD Place the onion, carrot, and celery with the grapeseed oil in a medium saucepan and sauté over medium heat for 7 minutes, or until caramelized. Add the tomato and pour in the red wine to deglaze the pan. Cook until most of the wine has been absorbed. Add the Game Bird Stock and cook over low heat for 1 hour, or until reduced to 1 cup. Strain through a fine-mesh sieve.

Meat or Game Stock

This recipe can be used for any type of meat or game stock, including beef, hare, veal, venison, or lamb.

Yield: 2 quarts

6 pounds bones (such as beef, hare, veal, venison, or lamb)

2 cups chopped carrot

2 cups chopped celery

4 cups chopped Spanish onion

3 cloves garlic

2 tablespoons canola oil

1/2 cup chopped tomato

2 cups red wine

1 bay leaf

1 tablespoon peppercorns

METHOD Preheat the oven to 450 degrees. Place the bones in a roasting pan and roast for 1 hour, or until golden brown. Turn the bones after 30 minutes to ensure even browning.

Place the carrot, celery, onion, and garlic with the canola oil in a large stockpot and sauté over medium-high heat for 7 minutes, or until caramelized. Add the tomato and cook for 2 minutes. Deglaze the pan with the red wine and cook until most of the wine has been absorbed. Add the browned bones, bay leaf, and peppercorns and cover with cold water. Bring to a boil, reduce the heat to medium-low, and simmer slowly, uncovered, for 6 to 8 hours, or until reduced to 2 quarts, periodically skimming the impurities that rise to the surface. Strain through a fine-mesh sieve. Store in the refrigerator for up to 4 days or freeze for up to 2 months.

Meat or Game Stock Reduction

This recipe can be used for any type of meat or game stock, including beef, hare, veal, venison, or lamb.

Yield: 1 1/2 cups

2 cups chopped Spanish onion

1 cup chopped carrot

1 cup chopped celery

2 tablespoons canola oil

1 cup red wine

1 1/2 quarts Meat Stock (such as beef, hare, veal, venison, or lamb)

4 sprigs thyme

METHOD Place the onion, carrot, and celery with the canola oil in a medium saucepan and sauté over high heat for 10 minutes, or until golden brown and caramelized. Deglaze the pan with the red wine and cook until most of the red wine has been absorbed. Add the Meat Stock and simmer for 1 hour. Strain, return to the saucepan with the thyme, and simmer for 5 minutes. Remove the thyme and simmer for about 30 minutes, or until reduced to about 1 1/2 cups. Strain through a fine-mesh sieve. Store in the refrigerator for up to 4 days or freeze for up to 2 months.

Mushroom Stock

Yield: 1 1/2 quarts

1 pound button mushrooms, cleaned

2 portobello mushrooms, cleaned

1 cup shiitake mushrooms, cleaned

1 cup chopped Spanish onion

1 bulb garlic, peeled
3 sprigs thyme
3½ quarts water

METHOD Combine all of the ingredients in a large stockpot and simmer for 1½ hours. Strain through a fine-mesh sieve. Store in the refrigerator for up to 4 days or freeze for up to 2 months.

Red Wine Jus

Yield: 1½ cups

1½ cups chopped Spanish onion
1 cup chopped carrot
1 cup chopped celery
2 tablespoons canola oil
1 Granny Smith apple, chopped
1 orange, peeled and chopped
6 cups Burgundy
3 cups Port

METHOD Place the onion, carrot, and celery in the canola oil in a medium saucepan and sauté over high heat for 10 minutes, or until golden brown and caramelized. Add all the remaining ingredients and simmer over medium heat, uncovered, for 1 hour. Strain through a fine-mesh sieve and return to the saucepan. Simmer for 30 to 45 minutes, or until reduced to 1½ cups.

Red Wine Reduction

This recipe can also be made with all Port for a Port Reduction.

Yield: 1 cup

1 cup chopped Spanish onion
½ cup chopped carrot
1 leek (white part only), chopped
1 tablespoon grapeseed oil
1 Granny Smith apple, chopped
6 cups Merlot
3 cups Port

METHOD Place the onion, carrot, and leek with the grapeseed oil in a medium saucepan and sauté over high heat for 10 minutes, or until golden brown and caramelized. Add all the remaining ingredients and simmer over medium heat, uncovered, for 1 hour. Strain through a

fine-mesh sieve and return to the saucepan. Simmer for 30 to 45 minutes, or until reduced to 1 cup.

Red Wine–Shellfish Emulsion

Yield: 1 cup

1 Spanish onion, coarsely chopped
1 carrot, coarsely chopped
1 stalk celery, coarsely chopped
1 Granny Smith apple, coarsely chopped
2 cloves garlic
2 tablespoons grapeseed oil
1 750-ml bottle Merlot
2 cups Shellfish Stock (see below)
¼ cup butter
Salt and pepper

METHOD Cook the onion, carrot, celery, apple, and garlic in the grapeseed oil in a medium saucepan over medium heat for 15 minutes, or until golden brown. Add the Merlot and simmer for 2 hours. Strain and place in a small saucepan with the Shellfish Stock. Simmer over medium heat for 1 hour, or until reduced to 1 cup. Whisk in the butter and season to taste with salt and pepper. Froth with a handheld blender just prior to serving.

Shellfish Stock

Yield: approximately 2 quarts

5 pounds lobster shells
½ cup chopped carrot
½ cup chopped Spanish onion
½ cup chopped celery
½ cup chopped leek
2 tablespoons grapeseed oil
3 tablespoons tomato paste
1 cup Burgundy

METHOD Preheat the oven to 400 degrees. Place the lobster shells in a roasting pan and roast for 40 minutes, or until bright red and slightly golden brown.

Place the carrot, onion, celery, and leek with the grapeseed oil in a large, deep pan and sauté over medium-high heat for 7 to 8 minutes, or until golden brown and caramelized. Add the tomato paste and

cook for 2 to 3 minutes. Deglaze the pan with the Burgundy and cook for 3 minutes, or until most of the Burgundy has been absorbed. Add the lobster shells and cover with cold water. Bring to a boil, reduce the heat to medium, and simmer, uncovered, for 3 hours. Strain through a fine-mesh sieve, discard the solids, and cook, uncovered, over medium heat for 30 to 45 minutes, or until reduced to 2 quarts. Store in the refrigerator for up to 4 days or freeze for up to 2 months.

Vegetable Stock

Yield: 2 quarts

1 cup chopped Spanish onion
1 cup chopped carrot
1 cup chopped celery
1 cup chopped fennel
1 red bell pepper, seeded and chopped
3 cloves garlic
½ cup chopped parsnip
1 bay leaf
4 quarts water

METHOD Place all the ingredients in a stockpot and bring to a boil. Reduce the heat to low and simmer, uncovered, for 1 hour. Strain through a fine-mesh sieve and cook over medium heat for 30 to 45 minutes, or until reduced to 2 quarts. Store in the refrigerator for up to 4 days or freeze for up to 2 months.

Other

Crispy Pig's Foot

Yield: approximately ½ cup

1 whole pig's foot
4 teaspoons grapeseed oil
½ cup chopped Spanish onion
½ cup chopped carrot
½ cup chopped celery
3 to 4 cups Chicken Stock (see page 227)

METHOD Preheat the oven to 350 degrees. Sear the pig's foot in 2 teaspoons of the grapeseed oil in a medium roasting pan over medium-high heat for 2 minutes on each side. Add the onion, carrot, and celery and cook for 5 to 7 minutes, or until caramelized. Add enough Chicken Stock to cover the pig's foot and roast for 2½ hours.

Remove the pig's foot from the liquid, remove the meat from the bone, and chop into small pieces. Heat the remaining 2 teaspoons of the grapeseed oil in a small sauté pan and add the meat. Cover and cook over high heat for 1½ minutes. Turn the meat over and cook for 1½ minutes. Remove from the pan and chop into small pieces.

Curry Butter

Yield: ½ cup

¼ cup peeled, chopped Granny Smith apple
1 clove garlic
1 shallot, chopped
1 teaspoon canola oil
2 teaspoons curry powder
½ teaspoon paprika
2 tablespoons water
¼ cup butter, softened

METHOD Place the apple, garlic, and shallot with the canola oil in a small sauté pan and sauté over medium heat for 7 minutes, or until the apple is tender. Add the curry powder, paprika, and water and cook for 3 minutes. Let cool and fold in the butter. Purée until smooth and strain through a fine-mesh sieve. Refrigerate until ready to use or for up to 3 days, or freeze for up to 2 months.

Herb Pasta

This recipe can be used for any type of herb pasta, including cilantro, parsley, or sage.

Yield: approximately 12 ounces

1 cup extra-fine semolina flour
2 eggs, lightly beaten
*½ cup loosely packed fresh herbs
(such as cilantro, parsley, or sage)*

METHOD Place the flour and eggs in the bowl of an electric mixer and mix on low speed with the paddle attachment for 3 minutes, or until the dough comes together. Form the dough into a ball and cover with plastic wrap. Refrigerate for at least 1 hour before rolling out.

Cut the herbs into a wide chiffonade. Roll out the pasta to the thinnest setting on a pasta machine. Sprinkle the herbs along half the length of the pasta and fold the other half over the herb-sprinkled half. Run through the pasta machine once more, or roll by hand until thin, to seal the herbs in the pasta.

Oven-Dried Apple Chips

Yield: 10 apple chips

2 cups water
1 cup sugar
¼ cup freshly squeezed lemon juice
10 paper-thin slices red apple

METHOD Preheat the oven to 225 degrees. Bring the water, sugar, and lemon juice to a simmer, stirring to dissolve the sugar. Add the apple slices and simmer for 10 minutes, or until the slices are translucent. Remove the apple slices from the liquid and lay them flat on a silpat-lined sheet pan. Bake for 1 hour, or until the apples are thoroughly dry. Carefully transfer the chips to a cooling rack. Store in an airtight container at room temperature until ready to use, or for up to 3 days.

Oven-Dried Pear Chips

Yield: 12 chips

½ cup sugar
½ cup water
12 ⅛-inch-thick slices pear, skin on

METHOD Preheat the oven to 225 degrees. Place the sugar and water in a small saucepan and cook over medium heat for 5 minutes. Add the pear slices and cook for 3 minutes, or until translucent. Drain and place on a silpat-lined sheet pan. Bake for 3 hours, or until dry to the touch. Remove from the pan while still warm, cool, and store in an airtight container until ready to serve.

Pickled Lamb Tongue

Yield: 1 tongue

1 lamb tongue
2 tablespoons chopped celery
2 tablespoons chopped Spanish onion

2 tablespoons chopped carrot
1 clove garlic
1 tablespoon rendered bacon fat
1 teaspoon grated fresh ginger
4 allspice berries, toasted
3 tablespoons brown sugar
⅓ cup rice vinegar
⅔ cup Chicken Stock (see page 227)
½ teaspoon salt

METHOD Soak the tongue in repeated changes of cold water for 1 day. Cook the celery, onion, carrot, and garlic in the bacon fat in a small saucepan over medium-low heat for 5 minutes, or until softened. Add the tongue and brown lightly on all sides, about 15 minutes. Add all the remaining ingredients, bring to a boil, and simmer for 2 to 3 hours, or until very tender. Cool in the liquid. Peel off the skin and trim away any gristle. The tongue may be used immediately or refrigerated for up to 1 week.

Pickling Juice

Yield: 2 cups

1 cup water
½ cup rice wine vinegar
½ cup plus 2 tablespoons sugar
2 tablespoons kosher salt
1 whole clove
1 teaspoon mustard seeds
1 teaspoon peppercorns
1 teaspoon chopped fresh ginger
½ jalapeño chile, seeded and chopped

METHOD Combine all of the ingredients in a saucepan and simmer for 5 minutes, or until the salt and sugar dissolve. Let cool, strain, and use as needed.

Potato Purée

Yield: 2 pounds

*1½ pounds Yukon Gold potatoes,
peeled and chopped*
Salt and pepper
1 cup milk, hot
½ cup butter

METHOD Cook the potatoes in boiling salted water for 15 to 20 minutes, or until tender. Drain and pass through a ricer. Place in a medium bowl, add the milk and butter, and whip until smooth. Season to taste with salt and pepper.

Preserved Ginger

Yield: about ¾ cup

1 cup finely julienned fresh ginger
1½ cups Simple Syrup (see below)

METHOD Blanch the ginger in simmering water for 3 minutes. Strain and repeat the process 2 more times. Simmer the ginger in the Simple Syrup for 30 minutes. Remove from the heat and cool in the syrup. Refrigerate in the syrup until needed.

Roasted Garlic

Yield: about ¾ cup

4 bulbs garlic, tops cut off
3 cups milk
½ cup olive oil

METHOD Preheat the oven to 350 degrees. Simmer the garlic bulbs and milk in a small saucepan for 10 minutes. Drain and discard the milk. Place the garlic bulbs upright in a small ovenproof pan and add the olive oil. Cover with a tight-fitting lid or aluminum foil and bake for 1½ hours, or until the garlic bulbs are soft.

Cool the garlic in the oil and then squeeze the soft garlic out of the skins. Use the garlic in cloves or purée the garlic and the oil until smooth.

Roasted Mushrooms

This recipe can be used for any type of mushroom, including cinnamon cap, black trumpet, shiitake, porcini, or matsutake.

Yield: 1½ cups

2½ cups mushrooms (such as cinnamon cap, black trumpet, shiitake, porcini, or matsutake), cleaned and stems removed
2 sprigs thyme or rosemary
½ cup chopped Spanish onion
1 tablespoon olive oil
⅓ cup water
Salt and pepper

METHOD Preheat the oven to 325 degrees. Place the mushrooms, herb sprigs, onion, olive oil, and water in an ovenproof pan and season with salt and pepper. Cover and roast for 30 to 40 minutes, or until the mushrooms are tender. Cool in the juices and refrigerate for up to 4 days.

Simple Syrup

Yield: 1½ cups

1½ cups sugar
1½ cups water

METHOD Combine the sugar and water in a small saucepan. Bring to a boil, stirring frequently, until all of the sugar is dissolved. Refrigerate until ready to use or for up to 1 month.

Glossary

BATON A cut the size of a wooden matchstick (⅛ by ⅛ by 2 inches).

BITTER MELON A popular ingredient in southern China and in Southeast Asia, this bitter-tasting vegetable, which is sometimes called fruit, resembles a bumpy-skinned cucumber.

BLACK CHICKEN This chicken, prized in Asia, has a more intense flavor than regular chicken.

BLACK PIG A black-haired pig that is generally raised on a diet of cream and apples.

BLANCHING AND SHOCKING To plunge a food into boiling salted water briefly and then to immediately place it into ice water to stop the cooking. Often used to firm the flesh or loosen the skins of such fruits as peaches or tomatoes. Also used to heighten and set color and flavor of herbs and greens.

BLEEDING HEART RADISH A radish with rosy pink flesh, green-and-pink skin, and flavor that is a cross between a turnip and a radish.

BLOOM To dissolve gelatin in water.

BRUNOISE A very fine dice, approximately ⅛ inch square.

BUDDHA'S HAND A large, misshapen citrus fruit with fingerlike protrusions around its sides. It is valued for its aromatic yellow-green skin, which is usually candied. The fruit contains little or no pulp or juice.

BURGUNDY CARROT A small, round burgundy-colored carrot with a slightly milder flavor than a regular carrot.

BURMESE RED RICE A reddish brown long-grain rice grown in Myanmar (formerly known as Burma). It requires more water and a longer cooking time than white rice.

CAPER BERRY Pickled caper fruit that resembles a coarse green grape, has a seedy, slightly starchy texture reminiscent of okra, and carries a flavor similar to that of the caper bud but less intense.

CHESTNUT This fruit from the chestnut tree must be cooked before eating. To cook, cut an X on one end of the chestnut and place in a 400-degree oven for 10 to 15 minutes, or until the skin begins to curl away from the nut. Remove from the oven and peel while still warm.

CHICKEN MUSHROOM Medium-sized mushroom with a brown cap, white stalk, and a mild flavor.

CHICKEN OYSTER The flesh that lies in the cup-shaped piece of bone at the top of the chicken thigh.

CHIFFONADE Fine strips, about 1/16 inch wide. Usually used in reference to leafy vegetables or herbs, which are rolled up and finely sliced.

CINNAMON CAP MUSHROOM Small mushroom with an orange-brown cap about the size of a nickel and a mild, earthy flavor.

CROSNE A slender beehive-shaped tuber with a flavor that is reminiscent of a sunchoke; popular in France.

CRU French for "growth." A term used to denote levels of quality in French vineyards, including cru classé, grand cru, and premier cru.

FIDDLEHEAD FERN Young, tightly coiled, edible fern frond.

FLEUR DE SEL Fine, light, snowy flakes of French salt harvested through the evaporation of sea water without the use of chemicals.

FRENCH GREEN LENTIL Tiny gray-green lentil with a yellow interior.

FRENCHED Excess fat and all meat and tissue removed from the bone, leaving the eye muscle intact, on a roast, rack, or chop.

FRIED CHICKEN MUSHROOM Medium-sized mushroom with a brown cap, white stalk, and a mild flavor.

GELATIN SHEET A sheet of gelatin, commonly used in Europe, is sold at some specialty food shops. If unavailable, substitute 1 teaspoon powdered gelatin for each leaf of sheet gelatin.

GOOSENECK YELLOW SQUASH A yellow summer squash with thin skin, moist flesh, and a mild flavor.

GRAPESEED OIL Oil from pressed grapeseeds that is neutral in flavor and has a high smoke point.

GREEN GARLIC Young garlic that has long green leaves, a small, soft bulb, and a very mild garlic flavor.

GREEN TEA NOODLES Noodles made from wheat flour, buckwheat flour, and dried green tea.

GROUSE Found primarily in Great Britain, a game bird that is similar to a quail. It has dark red flesh with a rich, gamy flavor.

HEDGEHOG MUSHROOM Wild, creamy yellow mushroom with firm flesh and a tangy flavor.

HEN OF THE WOODS MUSHROOM Large wild mushroom with a reddish orange cap, slightly chewy texture, and mild flavor.

HIJIKI SEAWEED A rich, chewy, full-flavored seaweed. It cannot be purchased fresh, but is readily available dried at Japanese and other Asian markets.

HORNED MELON Spiny yellow fruit with green pulp surrounding a pocket of seeds. To separate the pulp from the seeds, pulse once in a food processor and pass through a fine-mesh sieve.

ISRAELI COUSCOUS Large-grain couscous, first manufactured in Israel and now made throughout the Middle East. Rinse before and after cooking.

LARDON A long, thin strip of fat.

MATSUTAKE MUSHROOM A large mushroom that grows wild on pine trees in Japan.

MATSUZAKA BEEF Beef from cows raised in Matsuzaka, Japan, on a diet of sake-marinated rice, resulting in meat that is tender and full flavored.

MIRIN A sweet, low-alcohol Japanese cooking wine.

MUSCOVY DUCK A type of domesticated duck prized for its meaty breasts.

OROBLANCO Developed at the University of California, this pomelo-grapefruit cross has a sweet flesh.

PIG EAR MUSHROOM Medium-sized yellow-brown mushroom with wavy edges and one side of the cap higher than the other. It has white flesh and a mild, earthy flavor.

PINK PEPPERCORN FLAKES Crushed from the dried berry of a South American rose plant.

POM POM MUSHROOM White to light brown mushroom with a mild flavor and soft texture. It grows on conifer branches, from which it hangs in clusters that resemble a cheerleader's pom poms.

POULARD A neutered, fattened hen.

QUENELLE An oval dumpling made from a forcemeat of fish, veal, or poultry. By extension, the term is also used to mean the typical oval shape.

RAMP A wild onion that resembles a baby leek with broad leaves.

RICE BEANS Small white beans that, when dry, are slightly larger than a cooked rice kernel. They have a delicate skin and sweet flavor.

SCOTTISH HARE Larger variety of rabbits that get their flavor from the berries they eat.

SHEEP'S MILK MAPLE YOGURT Maple-flavored yogurt made from sheep's milk. It is available at specialty food stores.

SHISO LEAF A member of the mint family with a somewhat tangy lemon-mint flavor that is used primarily in Japanese cooking.

SWEAT To cook slowly over medium or low heat with very little fat until soft or translucent.

SZECHUAN PEPPERCORNS Hot, woodsy dried berries of an ash tree native to western China.

TAMARI SOY SAUCE A dark soy sauce, somewhat thicker and stronger than other soy sauces. Used in Asian cooking as a dipping or basting sauce.

TATSOI A tender green with small, round leaves and a mild flavor.

TINKER BELL PEPPERS Tiny, red sweet peppers.

TOGARASHI Dried chiles used as a seasoning in Japanese cooking.

TOMATO CONCASSÉ Peeled, seeded, and diced tomato.

TONBURI The seed of broom cypress from the Hanawa area of Japan. Called "land caviar" in Japan because it has a biting texture similar to caviar. It has a flavor reminiscent of green vegetables.

TRUFFLE A subterranean fungus highly prized for its pungent aroma and flavor; found primarily in certain regions of France and Italy. If fresh truffles are unavailable, substitute frozen truffles. Scrub lightly but thoroughly before using. White truffles are rarer and more expensive than black. Olive oils that have been infused with the highly pungent white truffle are available in gourmet shops.

VERJUS The delicately tart and refreshing unfermented liquid that results from crushing green grapes in midsummer when acid levels are high and sugar levels are low.

WATER CHESTNUTS Fresh water chestnuts are far superior to the canned, so accept no substitute. Boil for 10 minutes and peel before using. Available in many Asian markets.

continued from page 42

pepper. Place some of the watercress, salsify, and julienned apple over the mousse. Place a tuile over the apple and continue layering with the mousse, watercress, salsify, and apple and top with a second tuile. Spoon the vinaigrette around the plate and sprinkle with the lemon verbena.

Crispy Potato Tuiles

Yield: 32 tuiles

1 Idaho potato (about 10 ounces), baked and peeled
3 tablespoons butter
4 egg whites
2 tablespoons fresh flat-leaf parsley chiffonade
Salt and pepper

METHOD Preheat the oven to 300 degrees. Place the warm potato in a mixing bowl with the butter and the egg whites. Using an electric mixer fitted with the paddle attachment, mix on medium speed for 3 to 4 minutes, or until smooth. Pass the potato mixture through a fine-mesh sieve, fold in the parsley, and season to taste with salt and pepper.

Cut a template, making a 1½-inch round in the center of a thin piece of cardboard. Place the template on a nonstick sheet pan, spread a thin layer of the potato batter in the opening, and remove the template. Repeat until you have 32 tuiles. Bake for 12 to 15 minutes, or until golden brown. Remove the tuiles from the pan and cool.

Substitutions

Squab, chicken, salmon, bass

Wine Notes

Kammerner Heiligenstein Gruner Veltliner from Hirsch in the Kamptal district of Austria is an electric pairing with this dish. The white pepper character of the Gruner Veltliner is like a firecracker in the mouth, cutting through the candylike brandied apple and orange in the chicken liver mousse. The rich mouthfeel of the wine also makes it a lovely companion for the terrine.

---

continued from page 128

mushrooms, seasoning after each layer. Reserve any excess spinach for the leek emulsion. Firmly press down on the terrine with your fingers or a small wooden board. Fold the excess plastic wrap over the terrine and refrigerate for 3 hours, or until set.

Remove the terrine from the mold and rewrap tightly in plastic wrap. With the plastic wrap on, cut the terrine into 16 slices. Lay the slices on a parchment-lined sheet tray and remove the plastic wrap. Season with salt and pepper. Just prior to serving, flash the terrine slices in the oven for 1 to 2 minutes to remove the chill.

To prepare the parsnip purée: Place the parsnips in a small saucepan and cover with water. Simmer over medium heat for 20 minutes, or until very tender. Purée the parsnips with 3 tablespoons of the butter

and enough of the cooking liquid to create a smooth sauce. Season with salt and pepper.

To prepare the leek emulsion: Sweat the leeks with the remaining 4 tablespoons of the butter in a small sauté pan over medium heat for 5 to 7 minutes, or until tender. Add ¾ cup of the Vegetable Stock and simmer over low heat for 10 to 15 minutes, or until very soft. Refrigerate the leeks and their cooking liquid until chilled. Purée the leeks with the cooking liquid and ¼ cup of the reserved spinach and strain through a fine-mesh sieve. Place the purée in a small saucepan and add the remaining ¼ cup Vegetable Stock. Cook over medium heat for 5 minutes, or until warm. Season to taste with salt and pepper. Froth with a handheld blender just prior to serving.

ASSEMBLY Spoon the parsnip purée on each plate in a zigzag pattern. Place a slice

of each terrine on each plate. Arrange some of the julienned truffle, peppercress sprouts, and pickled salsify at opposite points of the beef cheek terrine. Drizzle the olive oil over the truffles, and spoon the leek emulsion over the base of the pheasant terrine.

Substitutions

Chicken, turkey, beef, oxtail, veal

Wine Notes

Two very different terrines are tied together by the silky leek emulsion and the bitter endive. Bruno Clair's Marsannay Rosé acts as a harmonizing element with its dry Pinot Noir fruit. The sweet, smoky flavors from the pheasant, beef cheek, and black truffle vinaigrette can handle something a bit fuller. Savigny-les-Beaune from Ecard maintains the same bright, upfront fruit but contributes a little more weight.

Photography Index

Index

©2001 by Charlie Trotter
Recipe photography ©2001 by Tim Turner
Location photography ©2001 by Michael Voltattorni

All rights reserved. No part of this book may be
reproduced in any form, except brief excerpts for the purpose of review,
without written permission of the publisher.

Ten Speed Press
P.O. Box 7123
Berkeley, California 94707
www.tenspeed.com

Distributed in Australia by Simon and Schuster Australia,
in Canada by Ten Speed Press Canada,
in New Zealand by Southern Publishers Group,
in South Africa by Real Rooks,
in Southeast Asia by Berkeley Books, and
in the United Kingdom and Europe by Airlift Book Company.

Project Coordinator and General Editor: Judi Carle, Charlie Trotter's
Editor: Aaron Wehner, Ten Speed Press
Copyeditor: Sharon Silva
Research, development, and recipe testing:
Sari Zernich, Charlie Trotter's

Design by Trope : Communication by Design, Oak Park, Illinois
Typeset in Monotype Walbaum by Paul Baker Typography, Inc., Chicago

Library of Congress Cataloging-in-Publication Data

Trotter, Charlie.
Charlie Trotter's meat & game / Charlie Trotter;
wine notes by Belinda Chang; food photography by Tim Turner.
p.   cm.
Includes bibliographical references and index.
ISBN 1-58008-238-6

1. Cookery (Meat) 2. Cookery (Game)
I. Title: Charlie Trotter's meat and game. II. Charlie Trotter's (Restaurant) III. Title.
TX749.T76 2001
641.6'6—dc21   2001002474

Printed in China by C&C Offset Printing Co., Ltd.
First printing, 2001

1 2 3 4 5 6 7 8 9 10 — 05 04 03 02 01